THE ROMANS

Bernardo Rogora
Illustrations
Studio Inklink, Sergio, G. Soriani

BARRON'S

DoGi

English translation © Copyright 1999 by Barron's Educational Series, Inc.
Original edition © 1999 by DoGi spa, Florence, Italy
Title of original edition: *I Romani*
Italian edition by: Bernardo Rogora
Illustrations by: Alessandro Bartolozzi; Lorenzo Cecchi; Inklink, Florence; Andrea Ricciardi; Claudia Saraceni; Sergio; Giacomo Soriani
Editor: Andrea Bachini
Graphic Design: Sebastiano Ranchetti
Page make-up: Laura Ottina
English translation by Paula Boomsliter for Lexis, Florence

All inquiries should be addressed to:
Barron's Educational Series, Inc.
250 Wireless Boulevard
Hauppauge, New York 11788
http://www.barronseduc.com

Library of Congress Catalog Card No. 99-66114

International Standard Book No. 0-7641-0949-9

Printed in Italy
9 8 7 6 5 4 3 2 1

Table of Contents

THE RISE TO POWER

Between the eighth and the fourth centuries B.C., a small village of warrior farmers became a powerful city-state. During their rise to power, the Romans integrated other cultures, developed an efficient army and administrative system, and revealed their political acumen and legal flair.

When a community that started out as a small village becomes a powerful city-state, it inevitably begins to create noble origins for itself. As their empire grew, the Romans invented the myths of the founding of Rome, which legend dates back to April 21, 753 B.C. But there actually is no precise date of origin of this city; it was formed gradually from the progressive union of villages that already existed on the hills near the Tiber River in the region called Latium in central Italy. In the tenth century B.C., there was a settlement on the Palatine, the most easily defended of the hills overlooking the Tiber. In time, settlements were established on the other hills as well. As the plain below gained in importance as a crossroads of the trade routes, the

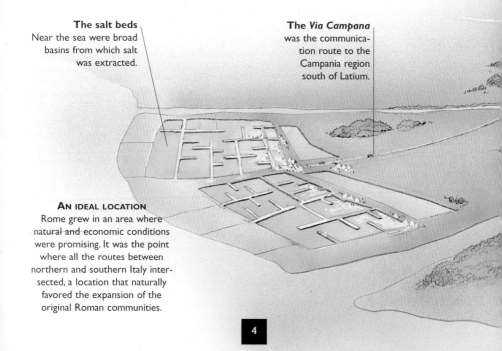

The salt beds
Near the sea were broad basins from which salt was extracted.

The *Via Campana*
was the communication route to the Campania region south of Latium.

AN IDEAL LOCATION
Rome grew in an area where natural and economic conditions were promising. It was the point where all the routes between northern and southern Italy intersected, a location that naturally favored the expansion of the original Roman communities.

independent hill communities expanded and gradually united. The Tiber was a decisive factor in this process; as with most other rivers in ancient times, it was a major communications link. About 12 miles (20 km) from its mouth on the Tyrrhenian Sea, the Tiber ran near some easily defensible hills. A small island made it easy to cross, and along its banks was flat terrain made fertile by the hard work of the community of villages. This extraordinary combination of natural features contributed to the formation of a trade center at the crossing of the river and the land-based routes on its banks. Three different ethnic groups—the Latins, the Sabines, and the Etruscans—lived in the area between the eighth and seventh centuries B.C.

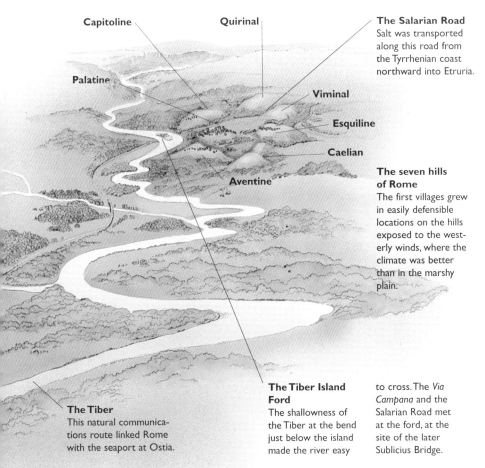

Capitoline

Quirinal

Palatine

Viminal

Esquiline

Caelian

Aventine

The Salarian Road
Salt was transported along this road from the Tyrrhenian coast northward into Etruria.

The seven hills of Rome
The first villages grew in easily defensible locations on the hills exposed to the westerly winds, where the climate was better than in the marshy plain.

The Tiber
This natural communications route linked Rome with the seaport at Ostia.

The Tiber Island Ford
The shallowness of the Tiber at the bend just below the island made the river easy to cross. The *Via Campana* and the Salarian Road met at the ford, at the site of the later Sublicius Bridge.

THE VILLAGE ON THE PALATINE was the original nucleus of the city of Rome. Rural and pastoral culture and customs were always the primary virtue of the Roman people, who were deeply attached to the land and to their rural origins.

The name "Rome" apparently derives from *rumon,* an Etruscan word meaning "river." Above: The Tiber at Tiber Island.

The market The site known as the Forum Boarium on the left bank of the Tiber, across from Tiber Island and at the ford in the river, hosted a trade emporium and later a market.

The first homes were circular huts made of wood with straw roofs. Each was surrounded by a ditch to permit rainwater to run off.

Clothing consisted of cloth tunics gathered at the waist with a leather belt or cloth band.

Agriculture
The Latins were herdsmen, hunters, and fishermen. Hard work invested in reclaiming and deforesting the plains below the hills permitted them to also make their living from agriculture.

Latin was spoken in Latium and later spread to the rest of Italy and the western parts of the Roman Empire. Originally, it was a mixture of terms from Greek and the other Indo-European languages spoken in the area. Right: Cippus of Perugia, an Etruscan legal/religious inscription. Museo Nazionale, Perugia.

The Latins

The Latins had settled between the lower part of the Tiber and the Alban hills at the beginning of the Iron Age, about 800 B.C. During the earlier Bronze Age, Latium was still subject to volcanic eruptions. The settlers were independent shepherds and farmers, and their villages established commercial relationships and had religious rites in common. The city of Alba Longa was the center of a league that celebrated solemn rites and sacrifices on Mount Cavo every year. In the eighth century B.C., Latium was mainly governed through small federations and religious alliances. The Latins also dealt with the Sabines, who from their native—and poorer—mountains had infiltrated the valleys and the hills populated by the more agriculturally advanced Latins. Sabine settlements existed in particular on the Quirinal and Viminal hills.

The Indo-Europeans

The Latins and the Sabines belonged to the great family of the Indo-European peoples. Italy of the eighth century B.C. was inhabited by a great variety of communities; among them, the peoples later called Italian were of Indo-European origin. The alphabet came to Italy in the eighth century B.C. Until that time, contrary to what had happened in the Aegean or Asia Minor, no great civilization had arisen on the peninsula. Politically, there were a great many city-states, culturally, a wide variety of ethnic groups and languages. It is commonly said

that Italy was a mosaic of different peoples. More than 20 Italian populations of Indo-European origin had settled in Italy before the first millennium B.C. Among these were the Greeks, whose colonists, from the eighth century B.C. on, founded prosperous cities in the southern part of the peninsula and shortly thereafter in Sicily; this was the great civilization of "Magna Graecia." Finally, there were the non-Indo-European peoples, first and foremost, the Etruscans.

Between myth and legend

It was in this varied panorama of different ethnic groups and cultures that

THE INDO-EUROPEANS
Since the 1800s, scholars in linguistics, archaeology, and history have been studying the origins and the features of this family of peoples that between the fifth and the second millennium B.C. made many migrations from the Volga steppes toward Europe and Asia.

The family
The social organization of the Indo-Europeans was based on clans, large extended families that descended from a single ancestor. The head of the family had absolute power.

The Indo-European peoples
Through great waves of migration, the Indo-Europeans merged with and supplanted earlier peoples to give rise to original civilizations: Albanian, Armenian, Baltic, Celtic, Dacian, German, Greek, Italian, Indian, Iranian, Macedonian, and Slavic.

Rome took its first steps in the eighth century B.C. The legends created by the Romans to attempt to add nobility to their origins recount how Rome was founded by Romulus, son of the god Mars and descendant of Aeneas, hero of the Trojan War, himself the son of the goddess Venus. The Roman people could thus boast that their origins were not only noble, but divine. All this has very little to do with historical facts. There never existed a Romulus who, after he received favorable omens in the form of a flight of birds, took his plow in hand and laid out the boundaries of the city. Also, Remus, who quarreled with his brother and was killed by him, is a product of the fertile

Religion consisted of the worship of natural forces. The Indo-Europeans worshipped such phenomena as lightning, fire, and rain, and their rites probably included making sacrifical offerings of sheep, pigs, and bulls to the gods.

A warrior society Almost everywhere, the Indo-Europeans imposed their warrior values and their superior military organization.

Social organization Family clans were grouped into tribes, each governed by a council of elders made up of the leaders of the clans. The king was elected from within the council.

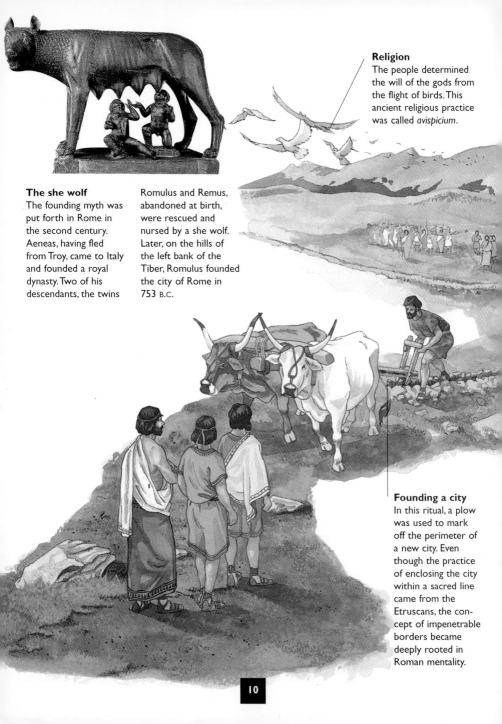

Religion

The people determined the will of the gods from the flight of birds. This ancient religious practice was called *avispicium*.

The she wolf

The founding myth was put forth in Rome in the second century. Aeneas, having fled from Troy, came to Italy and founded a royal dynasty. Two of his descendants, the twins Romulus and Remus, abandoned at birth, were rescued and nursed by a she wolf. Later, on the hills of the left bank of the Tiber, Romulus founded the city of Rome in 753 B.C.

Founding a city

In this ritual, a plow was used to mark off the perimeter of a new city. Even though the practice of enclosing the city within a sacred line came from the Etruscans, the concept of impenetrable borders became deeply rooted in Roman mentality.

City conservation
Sacrifices were performed in order to make the boundaries of the new city sacred and secure, and to thank the gods for having shown their will to the people.

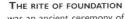

THE RITE OF FOUNDATION
was an ancient ceremony of Etruscan origin. The first phase involved consulation with the gods; the second, the delineation of the perimeter of the city; the third, a sacrificial celebration in the newly founded city.

imagination of the Romans. However, the legend is interesting because it perpetuates a ritual derived from the customs of the Etruscans, whose highly developed society so profoundly influenced ancient Roman culture.

The Etruscans

A true economic and military power, and a great culture—this defined the Etruscan people, who settled in what is now Tuscany and in northern Latium in the early years of the first millennium B.C. Soon, their dominion extended from the Po Valley in northern Italy to the Campania region in the south. The Etruscans were navigators and traders who lived in a land of bountiful farmlands and rich minerial deposits, in particular iron, copper, and tin. Their extraction enabled the Etruscans to become skilled metalworkers. Etruscan political organization was based on city-states, sometimes in confederations and sometimes at war with each other. Among the most important cities, all on highlands and well fortified, were Caere, Veii, Tarquinii, Vulcii, Rusellae, and Populonia. These were small independent states, each governed by a magistrate. The Etruscan cities never formed a strong unified state but remained divided politically. This weakness hastened their decline between the fifth and third centuries B.C., when they were forced to recognize the growing power of Rome.

The seven kings

Tradition has it that from 753 to 509 B.C. Rome was governed by seven kings: Romulus, Numa Pompilius, Tullus Hostilius, Ancus Marcius, Tarquinius Priscus, Servius Tullius, and Tarquinius Superbus. The last three are believed to have been Etruscans. This may be a legend, but one that contains some historical truths and sums up the important features of early Roman society and history. Early in history, in the hill villages, certain families emerged, due to the size of their flocks and their farmland. Most of the farmland was public property, at least in name, even though those who cultivated the lands had come to regard them as their own. A group of related "landed" families constituted a *gens* ("people"); the members used their given name and that of their *gens*. The heads of the families (*patres*) each held absolute power over their own people. They also elected the kings of Rome, who held religious powers and command of the armies. Only the legendary Romulus is said to have been Latin, and, according to tradition, his immediate successors were Sabines. Rome was originally a tolerant community, open to immigrants and the influences of new cultures.

The patricians

Over time, the power of the noble families grew stronger. The members of the Senate, the advisory body under the king, all came from their ranks. Possession of land, the ability to arm themselves to go to war, and the exercise of political power were the bases for the rise of the order of the patri-

Preparation
The ores extracted from the mines were broken up and selected by expert workers and placed in charcoal-heated stone furnaces.

MINING IN ETRURIA
The mining resources of Etruria were a crucial factor in the history of the Etruscans. The work involved in mining, from digging shafts and tunnels to carrying out the ore, was performed entirely with handmade tools: picks, hammers, mauls, chisels, and shovels. Mining and metallurgy were closely linked.

Metalworking

The art of modeling metals rose to heights of rare elegance in Etruscan society, as we see from the tools, weapons, and household objects found in their tombs. Left: Two plates flanking the head of a satyr. Below: An Etruscan chimera from the fourth century B.C.

The smelter

Here the metal was separated from the slag, which poured out of a special opening and was deposited on the bottom.

Casting

The purified metal was poured into molds and later finished to obtain such objects as weapons, jewelry, vases and containers, and plates and platters.

cians. It was a closed order and was initially unchallenged. Those who possessed less land needed the support of the patricians and contracted relationships of *clientela* or patronage with various patricians. They provided their patrons with services of every kind. These were the *clientes* (clients, or "those who serve"), who must not be confused with the plebeians, an order that was later formed. Farmers, citizens, and soldiers were the early patricians, soldiers who took their *clientes* to war with them. During the period of the first kings, Rome fought with the other cities of Latium, destroyed Alba Longa, increased in size, and consolidated its power over the region.

The Etruscan kings

The decisive turn of events in the transformation of Rome into a powerful city-state was the growth of power of the Etruscan kings. The influence of this civilization must be considered in light of the fact that in the seventh and sixth centuries B.C., Latium lay between the Etruscans of Tuscany and those of Campania. Consequently, the crossing of the Tiber at Tiber Island and linking up to the road network became increasingly important. The number of Etruscan traders and craftsmen in Rome increased. Of the Etruscan kings that tradition tells us reigned between 616 and 509 B.C., ancient historians have given us only three names, too few for the amount of time involved. For our purposes, however, it is more important to understand the changes that came about in that period in the

THE FAMILY
was the basic unit of Roman society and was headed by the father, whose power was tremendous and included even the right to kill or sell into slavery any members of his family.

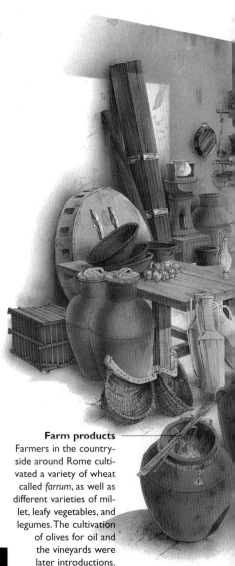

Farm products
Farmers in the countryside around Rome cultivated a variety of wheat called *farrum*, as well as different varieties of millet, leafy vegetables, and legumes. The cultivation of olives for oil and the vineyards were later introductions.

14

Slaves
In ancient Rome, debtors who could not repay the amounts they owed were made slaves.

Patricians
were farmers who cultivated the land. With the products of their labors they could afford the arms and armor needed to join the army.

Clients
The poorest of the plebeians entered the service of a patrician, for whom they performed all kinds of tasks without pay. In exchange, they were protected in those legal aspects of Roman life from which they were excluded by law.

Religion
The early Romans conceived of the gods as protectors of their families and the state. When the Romans came into contact with more advanced cultures—Etruscan and Greek—they identified many of their gods with the gods of these peoples. Right: a lararium or household shrine with the Genius (center) and the Lares, household divinities.

THE ARMY

In the early years of the monarchy, the army was composed solely of patricians and their clients. It is said that each of the 30 units supplied 100 infantrymen and 10 cavalrymen. Following the Servian reforms and the social division into the patrician and plebeian orders, the cavalry was made up of 18 equestrian centuries, and the infantry became the most important force. From the mid-fifth century B.C. on, three classes of citizens, inferior to the cavalry, made up the heavy infantry, while the two lowest classes formed the light infantry.

The centuries

The basis of Servius Tullius's reform was the division of the citizens into centuries, units established on the basis of wealth. There were 130 such centuries between the fifth and fourth centuries B.C. The centuriate organization first centered on army recruitment, but later took on political importance.

The light infantry

was made up of citizens in the lowest census class and consisted mainly of slingsmen and archers, whose equipment was less expensive.

 society, in the army, and in the urban structure of Rome. King Servius Tullius is attributed with many of the innovations that were to prove decisive for the future of Rome. The constant immigration of new and different peoples into Rome only reinforced its "openness"; by the sixth century B.C., without changing its Latin identity, immigration had made Rome the largest city in Latium and Etruria and one of the most powerful in Italy. The population had increased to about 35,000.

The Servian reforms

The first great turning point in Rome's history came when Roman citizenship

The cavalry was made up of men from the richest, most powerful classes, who could afford costly weapons and a horse.

The heavy infantry was made up of "middle-class" citizens equipped with both arms and armor.

The proletarians were the poorest class, who could not afford to outfit themselves and therefore provided only auxiliary services.

was granted to those who had settled in the territory of the city. The three ancient tribal divisions based on family origin were therefore replaced by territorial tribes. Membership in these tribes was decided on the basis of place of residence in the city or the location of one's lands in the surrounding territories. There were two reforms that were to prove important for the future of Rome: First, the census promoted by Servius Tullius classified all citizens according to income. Although it was mainly calculated in land, it nevertheless also took into account the value of a person's goods and the ownership of livestock and grain. The degree of one's wealth, not noble origin, became an indication of the strength of economic life and social organization in Rome at that time. The second great reform, concerning the organization of the army, was linked to the new way of classifying the Romans on a basis of wealth. A census was taken to determine how many were horsemen, how many would serve as infantrymen, and the number of people with no wealth who would perform auxiliary services. The extension of citizenship and the draft-

ing of all those who possessed the means to procure arms and armor permitted adopting the military tactic known as the "hoplite" formation, of Greek and Etruscan derivation. Infantry was lined up in close ranks and defended by large circular shields. The army was the expression of Roman power. The Romans were skillful in making use of all available human resources in the service of the city-state. Thanks to Rome's policy of welcoming foreigners, its military

Wall building
The walls were raised using blocks of a type of local stone called *cappellaccio*. The portions of the walls running over flat land were reinforced by a deep layer of fill of 98 to 131 feet (30 to 40 m).

THE SERVIAN WALLS
The building of the Servian walls around Rome was decreed by the military reforms of the sixth century B.C. Due to the vastness of the territory they enclosed, the walls represented a further element of social cohesion and contributed to creating unity within the city.

Extension
About 4 miles (7 km) of walls enclosed an area of about 703 acres (285 ha), one of the largest in the Italian world. Except for the Aventine, all the hills of Rome were within the Servian walls.

forces were able to grow to the extent that they soon outnumbered the forces of their neighbors. During the period of Etruscan rule, the urban structure of Rome changed drastically. Typical of these changes were the Servian walls and the Temple of Jupiter on the Capitoline Hill. The flat area of the forum was paved and became a center for public life. Rome thus became a united city, with buildings equal to those of the older cities of Etruria.

The birth of the republic and the plebeian class

In the late sixth century B.C., the elective monarchy was replaced by a republican regime headed by two consuls appointed on a yearly basis, but

A GRANDIOSE SCENARIO
The temples of the gods stood on the high terraced slopes and the city, in continual expansion, bustled with all types of activity.

The Temple of Jupiter Capitolinus, on the Capitoline Hill, was the most important in Rome. Dedicated to the Capitoline Triad (Jupiter, Juno, and Minerva), it stood at the edge of a steep cliff.

government was actually still dominated by the aristocrats. For the two centuries that followed, Rome was the center of conflicts between the patrician order and the new plebeian order. During the period of the Etruscan kings, foreign craftsmen and traders were integrated into Roman society and had elevated their standing in the favorable climate of economic growth and new construction. However, many Romans had become indebted, and lost their land holdings. Both groups were discontented, the former because of the limits imposed on their participation in political life, a privilege reserved for the patricians, and the latter due to their miserable condition. At the same time, the patricians, who had become dissatisfied with the monarchy, which

Roman homes were well built, with stuccoed walls and tiled roofs. The richest were adorned with terracotta ornaments

Rich decorations
The Italian people habitually embellished their private homes with wall decorations depicting natural or mythological subjects. Excellent, although late examples are the splendid mosaics of the Villa of Piazza Armerina in Sicily.

The Regia
Originally the home of the king, over time it became the home of the cult of Mars and Ops Consiva, a goddess of plenty and fertility.

they felt favored the emerging classes too much, began to consider overthrowing it and thus increasing their own power. In practical terms, that power excluded the plebeians from the distribution of conquered lands. The state of affairs was further aggravated by the possibility of insolvent debtors becoming slaves, and by the lack of written laws. Both those who were well off economically and those who were poor were unhappy with patrician power. Both groups became aware of their common interests, and this phenomenon coincided with the formation of the plebeian order.

Power to the plebs

Following the Servian reforms, the population was subdivided into groups, called centuries, on the basis of the census. Military responsibilities were assigned to each. Rich plebeians and all those who could afford the various types of military equipment played an important role in the army. Their refusal to fight and their threat of secession was therefore quite persuasive with the patricians. A few decades after the establishment of the republic, the struggle between patricians and plebs came to a head. In 494 B.C., the plebeians obtained the right to elect the holders of a new office, called the tribunes of the plebs, whose task it was to defend them. They held the right to veto the decisions of the two consuls who were elected annually to the top ranks of republican government. There were further repercussions regarding the competencies of

PROPERTY AND PROPRIETORS IN ROME

The economic and social history of Rome is linked to the land. Farming was the most important activity and the main source of wealth. To understand the economic development of Rome, it is important not to confuse ownership of the land, which in early Rome was very limited, with possession, that is, the ability of a family to work and exploit the land.

Land use
Initally, the aristocratic families worked the state land as if it were their own and integrated its products with those of their private land.

The patricians
Later, the state land was distributed among the patricians, who cultivated it and made good profits. In exchange, they were required to pay a tax to the state.

The plebeians
The exclusion of the plebeians from the distribution of state lands created discontent among this class.

The *fundus*
The first private property to exist in Rome was the home and the garden inside the city walls: the *fundus*. Right: A model hut. Antiquarium del Palatino, Rome.

The *compascua*
were state-owned lands around private farms. The farmers were allowed to freely graze their flocks in these pastures. Above and below: Scenes of rural life, sixth century B.C. Bardo Museum, Tunis.

Private land
The concession of limited private property in the territories around the city, the *ager privatus*, is said to have been instituted by Romulus himself.

Public land
As Rome grew and expanded to encompass the territories of conquered peoples, the term *compascua* was replaced by *ager publicus*, meaning public or state land.

THE *COMITIA CENTURIATA,* instituted in the fifth century B.C., was an assembly of great importance because they elected the consuls and the most important magistrates.

The fasces was a bundle of rods and a projecting axe that symbolized the power of the highest magistrates. It was carried by the lictor, an official of the magistrate's retinue.

The consuls, elected by the *comitia centuriata,* exercised the powers previously held by the king, although they had some limitations, such as having to win the approval of the Senate.

The Twelve Tables
marked the passage
from oral to written
law. The "tablets" are in
fact 12 sheets of
bronze on which the
first written laws were
engraved in 451 B.C.

the assemblies of the centuries. In 451 B.C., the office of the decemvir was created: ten men charged with laying down written law for the first time. These were the Laws of the Twelve Tables, which set down the laws in writing. In 445 B.C., the plebeians obtained the freedom to marry patricians, and by 336 B.C., they could be elected consuls. The complete equality of the two orders, which, however, applied only to male citizens, in practice benefitted only the rich plebeians, since participation in political life and public office was not salaried.

Power in Latium and the arrival of the Gauls

In the early years of the republic, Rome had to defend itself against the Etruscans and the cities of the Latin League that were worried by its growing power. In 493 B.C., a treaty among the Latin cities of the league established peace and called for providing reciprocal aid in the case of attack from other peoples. The Romans then fought against the Volsci and the Equi, and more than once against the Etruscan city of Veii, which wanted to control the lower part of the Tiber. When Veii finally fell, in 396 B.C., Rome had become the most formidable power in central Italy. But another threat soon appeared: the Gauls, nomadic warriors of Celtic origin, who came to Etruria in about 390 B.C. After having laid siege to the Etruscan city of Clusium (Chiusi), the Gauls headed for Rome. The Roman army met them

The magistrates
Many of the most important magistrates were elected by the *comitia centuriata*. The public offices they held were annual and collegial; a magistrate's mandate could not last more than one year and for each office at least two persons were elected and required to act by mutual agreement.

in combat but was routed; the frightened Romans abandoned their homes and left only a garrison in defense of the Capitoline. The troops resisted the assault of the Gauls, who had destroyed the rest of the city. All seemed lost, but the Gauls finally agreed to withdraw in exchange for a huge sum of money. The consequences of this raid were extremely serious. Besides its material losses, Rome watched helplessly as its military prestige and fame for invincibility, on which its supremacy in Latium was founded, crumbled. The Latins, in fact, rebelled, and even some Etruscan cities, such as Caere and Tarquinii, took advantage of the situation to attack from the north. But the Romans won out in the end. With great tenacity, they rebuilt their city, subjugated the Etruscans of Caere, and, in 358 B.C., even reinstated the Latin League. Following a series of wars that lasted almost 40 years, by 351 B.C. Rome had again consolidated its control over the Etruscans, the Latins, and the other peoples of central Italy.

THE CELTS
were nomadic warriors who appeared suddenly and spread out from the heart of Europe from the eighth to the fifth century B.C. The Celts were the first to exploit the salt and iron that was abundant in the mines of central Europe as commodities. The two main centers of development of the first Celtic civilization were Hallstatt in Austria and La Tène in Switzerland.

THE GAULS
The Celts later spread into France and Belgium where they mixed with the local tribes and gave rise to the Gallic people.

The Hallstatt salt mine
The rocks were flushed and the water channeled into special basins, which were heated by burning great quantities of wood. The water evaporated and the salt collected on the bottom of the basin.

Tomb furnishings
Objects found in tombs in the Hallstatt area—swords, daggers, lances, ceremonial containers—testify to the ability of the Celts as metalworkers and craftsmen.

THE CONQUEST OF THE MEDITERRANEAN

Between the fourth and third centuries B.C., Rome extended its dominion over the entire Mediterranean basin. After having conquered Italy, Rome went on to defeat its powerful adversary, Carthage; seize Greece, the center of the great Classical civilization; and subjugate Asia Minor.

The causes and the conditions that favored and accompanied Roman expansion can be found by examining Rome itself: the economy, the relationship between patricians and plebeians, the new forms of military organization, and Rome's intelligent policy regarding the territories it conquered.

Economy and society

The fourth century was a period of development for the Roman agricultural economy, and this depended in part on the limits imposed on the single farmers regarding use of the public land. New stimulus was given to the trade controlled by richer plebeians.

CIVIS ROMANUM SUM
For centuries, the phrase "I am a citizen of Rome!" gave power to those who could declare it truthfully. Strong men, used to having total command: this was how the Romans were portrayed even in unofficial portraiture. This head from Cerveteri, now in the Museo Romano di Villa Giulia, is but one example.

DIVIDE ET IMPERA!
"Divide and conquer!" was the motto of the Romans as they sowed discord among their enemies, lured more friendly populations into their fold, and put down rebels. Their strategy was also based on offerering specific conditions to the different conquered cities.

The federated cities
were governed by their own laws and magistrates and were bound to Rome by treaties of alliance that made their citizens allies of the Romans. The terms of alliance were not identical for all the cities.

The economic interests of a considerable part of Roman society turned toward military and political expansion into the south of Italy. With the newly rich as mediators, the conflicts between patricians and plebeians had been in part resolved through a series of agreements that culminated in the rise of the plebeians to posts in the city administration. Actually, there had arisen a new management elite formed of patricians and rich plebeians, a patrician-plebeian alliance. The less-well-to-do citizens saw an easing of the consequences of their widespread and deep indebtedness, which could lead debtors into slavery. The less-well-to-do plebeians became more fully integrated into the army. The hoplite formation was set aside and the closed-rank alignment

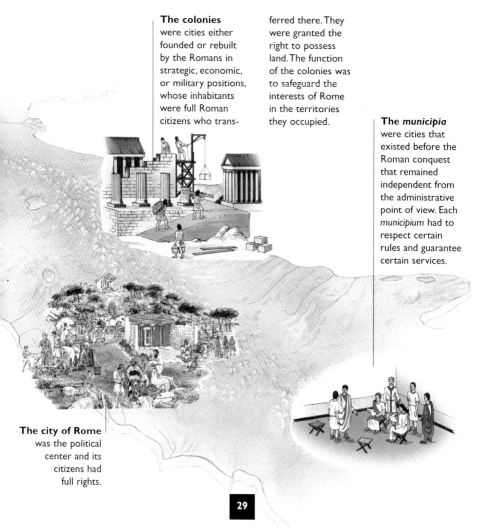

The colonies were cities either founded or rebuilt by the Romans in strategic, economic, or military positions, whose inhabitants were full Roman citizens who transferred there. They were granted the right to possess land. The function of the colonies was to safeguard the interests of Rome in the territories they occupied.

The *municipia* were cities that existed before the Roman conquest that remained independent from the administrative point of view. Each *municipium* had to respect certain rules and guarantee certain services.

The city of Rome was the political center and its citizens had full rights.

was replaced by a more agile tactic based on the array of troops in small divisions of 60 to 120 men. Also, the system used for enlisting soldiers was changed. Up to this time, the richest citizens, and therefore those equipped with the most costly arms and armor, had made up the greatest number of centuries, and this fact had forced each of them to perform more frequent periods of military service. But with the new enlistment system, based on membership in the territorial tribes, the army began using the plebs more efficiently. The founding of many new colonies in the territories conquered by the Romans also contributed to placating their demands. The colonies were destined to be populated by Roman citizen-soldiers. They were assigned a part of the surrounding land, even though it remained public land and property of the Roman state. Another fundamental element in Rome's expansionist policies was the Romans' extraordinary and original capacity to establish relationships with the territories they conquered, avoiding brutal repression. They assigned different roles to the cities and implemented an intelligent policy of involvement in the formation of the army through alliances and the enlistment of troops.

The Samnite Wars

The population of the colonies by Romans, the improved domestic political situation, and the renewed vigor of the army reinforced by the new plebeian forces permitted Rome to take immediate advantage of the great

THE CIVILIZATION OF MAGNA GRAECIA
Colonies founded by the Greeks in southern Italy expanded and prospered, with large amounts of trade and economic and cultural activities. The most important towns were Siracusa, Agrigento, Paestum, Reggio Calabria, Taranto, and Messina.

The agora
This public square was the center of social, political, economic, and cultural life. The population gathered here for religious celebrations and processions, to discuss politics, and to learn the latest news.

The temples
Built mainly in the Doric style, with wide channeled columns and sumptuous decoration, the temples were very impressive.

Religion
embraced the cults of both the gods and heroes such as Heracles or Theseus and was character-ized by great free-dom; each family had its own household god and each city its protector or protectress deity. Animal sacrifices were common practice on altars before the temples.

The works of art
The Romans, who had never thought much of art, were enchanted by the perfection and the beauty of Greek works. There is much truth in the statement that Roman art derives from the Greek models.

A NEW WORLD
The Greeks colonized the Mediterranean between the mid-eighth and the early fifth centuries B.C. Culture and art in the colonies saw the importation during this period of works and models from Greece, but Magna Graecia also developed a distinct colonial style.

Greek civilization
The refined and highly evolved Greek culture slowly spread to Rome, where it opened broad horizons for art, literature, science, and philosophy.

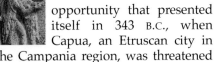

opportunity that presented itself in 343 B.C., when Capua, an Etruscan city in the Campania region, was threatened by the Samnites and requested aid. Together with the Latin League, the Romans rushed to the rescue, and thus began the Samnite Wars, which were to continue until 290 B.C. This was a period of harsh struggles, marked by three different wars. The conflicts concluded with victory for the Romans, who then subjected a vast territory composed of the dominions of the Samnites and their allies: the Senonian Gauls, Etruscans, Umbrians, Sabellians, and Lucanians. In 340 B.C., between the first and the second Samnite Wars, angered by Rome's refusal of their request for Roman citizenship, the Latins also took up arms. The Roman victory over the Latins two years later ended the Latin

League, and each city that had been party to it was bound to Rome by a separate treaty of alliance. This was a very clever move, since the Romans knew that if the subject cities united, they would represent a fearful foe. They therefore decided to stipulate particular forms of alliance separately with each city. The conditions and rights were different in each case and based on the opportunities offered by each of the single territories, on the real feelings of friendship and loyalty each had for Rome, and on the interests that bound each to the victorious city. After defeating the Samnites, Rome turned its eye to the flourishing cities of southern Italy.

Magnificent cities
The Temple of Athena at Paestum (about 510 B.C.). In the fertile plains were large, magnificent cities resplendent with temples, squares, votive altars, and buildings, all surrounded by mighty walls with square, polygonal, or circular towers. The streets bustled with activities of all kinds, from crafts to commerce.

Sculpture
The Greek temples were richly decorated with many types of sculpture. The spaces between the friezes of the Doric temples were often adorned with carvings. This example is from the Heraion at the mouth of the Sele River at Paestum (510–500 B.C.) and represents *Dancing Girls*.

The conquest of Magna Graecia

Tarentum (Taranto) offered Rome the opportunity it was looking for. A Roman garrison sent to aid the city of Thurii provoked the violent reaction of the Tarantines, who feared the consequences of Roman intervention and declared war. Rome was powerful and had a great army, so Taranto requested the aid of an able leader of men: Pyrrhus, king of Epirus (modern northern Greece). Pyrrhus dreamed of uniting and leading all the Greeks of southern Italy and Sicily in a great central Mediterranean maritime power capable of competing with Carthage in North Africa. He therefore welcomed the invitation, and in 280 B.C. arrived in Italy with a mighty army. In the beginning, he won some important victories, but he was not quite able enough to turn the tide in his favor, and Rome, assisted by the Carthaginians with whom an alliance had been formed, scored the decisive victory over Pyrrhus in 275 B.C. Pyrrhus then abandoned southern Italy, which was conquered by the Romans. The latter had fought and defeated the Lucanians, Brutti, and Samnites who had allied with the enemy. Therefore, in the second half of the third century B.C., central and southern Italy, from Rimini to the Strait of Messina, was under Roman control. From then on, Rome was to be considered one of the great Mediterranean powers. The city literally blossomed with new homes, temples, and public buildings. The policy initiative by Appius Claudius Caecus, who first gave literary form to

The Roman roads
The road system in Italy, and later in the provinces, was one of Rome's most glorious achievements. By the first century B.C., all of Italy was linked by excellent roads, built for strategic reasons. Normally, there was a city about every 18 miles (30 km), an average day's march for the Roman army. Many of today's highways follow the routes of the ancient Roman roads.

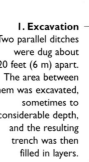

2. The *statumen* was the first layer, made up of rather large stones mixed with earth or sand.

1. Excavation
Two parallel ditches were dug about 20 feet (6 m) apart. The area between them was excavated, sometimes to considerable depth, and the resulting trench was then filled in layers.

ROAD BUILDING

Road building was a long and complex affair. Special attention was paid to the foundation, which was essential if the finished road were to endure.

4. The *pavimentum*
Over the *rudus* was laid a layer of gravel compressed to form a surface that was arched to permit good drainage. On the most important roads a final paved surface was added.

3. The *rudus* was a layer of pebbles held together with mortar. It was laid over the *statumen* and beaten with sledgehammers to obtain stability.

Milestones were distributed throughout the entire Roman road system and marked the distance from the closest major city. The distances were calculated in miles (one Roman mile was equal to 1,620 yards [1,481.75 m]). Right: A milestone in Val Pusteria, Alto Adige (Italy).

his speeches and is considered to be the first Latin prose writer, resulted, in about 310 B.C., in the construction of the first Roman aqueduct and of the first great military road, the *Via Appia*, linking Rome and Capua.

Other changes also loomed; the conquest of Magna Graecia and the new, direct contacts with Greek civilization finally permitted the Romans to learn its secrets. Until that time, Greek influence on Roman culture had been considerable but fragmentary, arriving, as it had, gradually through the merchants who traveled through Rome, and through Rome's dealings with the cities of the south. Direct contact, instead, provided an immediate, strong stimulus to the development of

Religion
The Carthaginians venerated Moloch, represented as a giant with the head of a bull, to whom they made human sacrifices.

THE PORT
In the third century B.C., Carthage reached the height of its splendor. Its port, defended by a formidable fleet, was an important center for the trade of finished products and raw materials.

Big business
Merchants traded products of every kind and origin, such as Carthaginian purple dye, ostrich plumes from central Africa, elephant tusks from Sudan, oil from Sicily, and enamels and rugs from Egypt.

Roman culture, which was still lacking a definite artistic and literary identity. From that time on, local culture in Rome began to flourish and progress.

Carthage, Rome's great rival

When Rome, with the conquest of the Magna Graecia, looked out triumphantly over the western Mediterranean, it naturally clashed with the interests of another great power, Carthage. This city, founded by the Phoenicians of Tyre in the ninth century B.C. on what is today the Gulf of Tunis, had used its strategic position to progressively gain control of the Mediterranean basin. Rich and determined, Carthage built up a wide-ranging African dominion that extended from the border of Cyrenaica (in Libya)

Access to the port
The entrance to the port of Carthage was about 69 feet (21 m) wide and closed by an iron chain.

to Gibraltar, as well as the southern Spanish coast, the Balearic Islands, Sardinia, Corsica, and western Sicily. Carthage was also a republic, but unlike Rome, its ruling class was made up of rich traders and powerful shipowners. Carthage, in fact, owed its wealth to the sea, trade, and the incredible volume of business conducted in its extraordinary port. But despite offering strong competition for Rome, Carthage had some weaknesses from the political and military points of view. The city had never granted any rights to the peoples it defeated, as Rome had, and its dominion therefore rested on less stable foundations. The army, mighty as it might have seemed, was made up of mercenaries instead of citizens fighting for their own country. Carthaginian commanders, on the other hand, were true professionals, unlike the Romans.

A brilliant idea
The inventor of the *corvus* was the consul Gaius Duilius, who thanks to this innovation defeated the Carthaginians at Mylae.

The *corvus*
was a plank about 26 feet (8 m) long with a beaked hook. It was thrown onto the enemy ships to permit the Romans to board.

The crew
was composed of 300 sailors (of whom 270 were oarsmen) and 120 "marines," with about 20 officials and petty officers.

The rowers
were arranged on three levels: two per oar on the upper levels and one per oar on the bottom level.

The battles on land went on for years because the great Carthaginian fleet guaranteed supplies to its troops. In order to end the war, the Romans were forced to build a fleet capable of destroying that of their enemy. They built and armed 100 quinquiremes and 20 triremes.

The quinquireme was a ship about 131 feet (40 m) long and from 20 to 23 feet (6 to 7 m) wide.

The First Punic War

The clash between Rome and Carthage began in 264 B.C. The opportunity arose when the Mamertines, Campanian mercenaries who had occupied Messina, found themselves in trouble and turned for help first to Carthage and then to Rome. The Romans occupied Messina and drove out the Carthaginians, starting the First Punic War, during which Rome conquered almost all of Sicily. Early on, however, the Romans realized the war could not be won without a fleet. They thus accomplished an extraordinary feat: In only two months, the Romans built a fleet of 120 ships, and defeated the Carthaginian navy at Mylae. A second naval victory off the Egadi Islands forced Rome's adversaries to surrender. The peace conditions imposed by the Romans called for Carthage's withdrawal from Sicily and payment of a huge indemnity in silver. The First Punic War had lasted 23 years. Sicily's cities were not afforded the status of ally, but were administered directly from Rome. Sicily became the first of Rome's provinces. Soon thereafter, the Romans also conquered Sardinia, Corsica, and Cisalpine Gaul, and also succeeded in expanding into Epirus.

The war against Hannibal

Defeat had been hard for Carthage to accept, and it set out to recoup its prestige and power as soon as possible. The city therefore turned to Spain, rich in silver mines and above all in a formidable strategic position from which to resume the inevitable war against

CROSSING THE ALPS
The Carthaginians' march through the difficult territory decimated their army. By the time he reached the Po Valley, Hannibal had lost 10,000 infantrymen, 6,000 cavalrymen, and most of his elephants.

Mission impossible
Hannibal's army faced incredible hardships in thwarting the Roman attempt to stop his march and also escaping attacks by the local populations.

The pass
It is still not clear which pass Hannibal crossed to enter Italy, but evidence points to its being the Monginevro.

Rome. Both powers could not exist together in the Mediterranean; one would have to succumb. The mission to Spain was entrusted to Hamilcar Barca, a general and member of one of Carthage's most influential families. He and his son-in-law and successor Hasdrubal conquered the Iberian coast from Gibraltar to the Ebro. In 221 B.C., Hamilcar died and his son Hannibal, an archenemy of the Romans, decided to test his strength against Rome. In 218 B.C., he took Saguntum, a city allied with Rome, and this started the Second Punic War. While Rome was preparing to deploy its legions to fight in Spain,

The elephants
The Carthaginians used elephants in battle, much as modern armies use armored tanks.

Hannibal's route
From Spain, Hannibal crossed France and the Alps to reach Italy. He then moved south, and from Crotone sailed for Zama.

Arausio
Roma
Cannae
Mare Internum
Crotone
Saguntum
Nova Carthago
Carthago
Zama

Hannibal, with incredible speed, crossed the Pyrenees and, after a march through France and over the Alps, descended into Italy. He caught the Romans completely unprepared. Rome would have been within easy reach, but Hannibal preferred heading south to persuade Rome's most important allies to join him. This was a serious mistake, so serious, in fact, as to decide the outcome of the war. It allowed the Romans time to organize their defenses and to prepare a counterattack. Quintus Fabius Maximus was elected dictator with full powers. His strategy consisted of a delaying tactic to tire the enemy, and to harass Hannibal's march with surprise attacks. He also avoided meeting the Carthaginians head-on on the battlefield, which he knew would have been fatal. At the end of Fabius Maximus's term, however, his successors decided to adopt

The legionary was a soldier. His basic fighting gear was a helmet, a sword, and chain-mail armor.

Scipio Africanus, Roman general and political figure, won decisive battles against the Carthaginians. At Zama, in northern Africa, he defeated Hannibal in 202 B.C. and so ended the Second Punic War.

The centurion was the leader of the century and was generally aided by another officer of inferior rank.

THE ROMAN ARMY
was made up of legions, which in the third century numbered about 4,200 men each. Each legion was divided into ten cohorts, each of which was subdivided into centuries.

War machines
were of different types, including rams, ballistas, and onagers. One machine feared by Rome's enemies was the catapult, which could launch stones weighing 220 pounds (100 kg).

The medics
The army was attended by physicians whose main activity was surgery. They were considered lower-rank officials and enjoyed various types of immunity. In some periods of Roman history there were even *valetudinaria*, or field hospitals.

exactly the opposite tactic, and in 216 B.C., on the battlefield of Cannae, in Apulia, the Romans suffered a disastrous defeat. Fabius Maximus's tactics were thus reinstated, and this time, not only against Carthage but also against the many Italian cities that had rebelled against Rome. In the meantime, all Hannibal's supply lines with Carthage had been severed, and the Romans had also opened another front in Spain. Commanding the troops was Publius Cornelius Scipio, who in a few years drove the Carthaginians from Spain and then, in order to force Hannibal out of Italy, landed in Africa and attacked Carthage directly. The Romans, led by Scipio, who later was known as Africanus, won the conclusive victory over Carthage in 202 B.C., at Zama. Carthage renounced all its possessions outside of Africa, paid a heavy cash indemnity, and pledged never again to declare war without authorization from Rome.

The conquest of the eastern Mediterranean

The victory over Carthage had made Rome well aware of its strength as a rich and powerful city. Rome's experience in far-off lands and its contacts with the most advanced of Mediterranean civilizations, everywhere under Hellenistic influence, provided a further stimulus to the new mentality that had first penetrated Rome at the time of the conquest of Magna Graecia. Roman conservatives opposed the spread of Hellenism, fearing that the new culture would undermine the ancient rural traditions and introduce corruption and lax morals. The universally acclaimed victor over Carthage, Scipio Africanus, who, by the glory of his exploits, took on the aura of a Greek hero, was fascinated by the new ideals. Scipio wanted Rome to expand toward Greece, toward the Hellenistic east he so admired. After having overcome the opposition of the conservatives, Scipio, urged on by public opinion, imposed his will. In a series of wars over a span of about 50 years, Rome subjugated Macedonia and Greece. Special treatment was reserved for Athens and Sparta, since these cities

Alexander's dream
Alexander wanted his empire to be united by a single Greek culture, with which all the subjects could identify. In a certain sense he succeeded; even though his far-reaching dominion broke up at his death, Greek culture spread everywhere, and thanks to contacts with many different civilizations, developed new forms. This marble portrait of Alexander is by the sculptor Lysippos and today is in the Louvre Museum in Paris.

Geography
All branches of science proceeded by leaps and bounds. Eratosthenes (right) drew the first map in the third century B.C.

Physics
Archimedes (left), born in Syracuse in 287 B.C., was a mathematician, physicist, and inventor. His sophisticated war machines used the principle of the lever to multiply the applied force.

Sculpture

The Nike of Samothrace (second century B.C.) is a master piece of the Hellenistic age, which produced exquisite works full of life and movement. Today, it is in the Louvre Museum in Paris.

Following the conquests of Alexander the Great and his death in 323 B.C., Greek culture expanded far beyond the border of Greece and the colonies. This age in the history of culture, art, and kingdoms headed by Alexander's successors is called Hellenism.

The Altar of Zeus at Pergamum

This gradiose monument (second century B.C.) was decorated with splendid friezes of the battle of heroes and giants.

The Hellenistic age

was marked by a lively economic life, expanding trade and exchanges of all kinds, and the growth of such splendid cities as Alexandria in Egypt, Antioch, and Pergamum in Asia Minor. Left: The second-century B.C. theater of Pergamum.

45

were so well known in Rome for their great heroes. They were considered allies even though they answered to the governor of Macedonia.

The Romans also created a protectorate in Asia Minor. In 133 B.C., King Attalus III of Pergamum named Rome the heir to his kingdom, which was incorporated into the empire as a province.

CULTURAL TOURISM
With their conquest of Greece, the Romans were in turn captured by this splendid culture and above all by its art. The grandiose Athens, full of extraordinary monuments, soon became a model of beauty for Rome.

The downfall of Carthage

Even as it expanded its dominions in the East, Rome continued to consolidate its lands in the West. A number of important questions were still undecided, such as what to do with Carthage. The Roman ruling class was increasingly convinced that their ancient rival should be completely eliminated. Marcus Porcius Cato, called the Censor, never missed an opportunity to remind

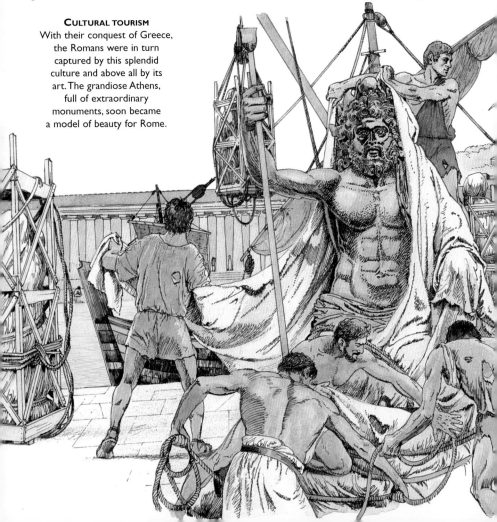

The Parthenon
The great temple dedicated to Athena, the Parthenon was built in the second half of the fifth century B.C. on the south side of the Athens acropolis. It was designed and built by the architects Icthynus and Callicrates under the direction of Pheidas, one of the most extraordinary artists in ancient times.

The works of art
Hundreds of master-pieces of Greek art were brought to Rome from the cities of Greece.

The ports
Greek wharves bustled with longshoremen and slaves who, before loading the statues, wrapped them to avoid damage during shipping.

Security measures
The works of art and sculptures were shipped to Rome mainly by sea and were usually guarded by Roman soldiers.

Viriathus
was a simple shepherd who became an outstanding general and inflicted great losses on the Roman armies in Spain.

REBEL POPULATION
Many peoples of the Iberian peninsula did not accept being ruled by Rome and were in continual revolt. Among them were the Celtiberians and the Lusitani.

Guerilla warfare
Viriathus put the guerilla technique to good use. With his perfect knowledge of the terrain, he waged war against the Romans, who were continually taken by surprise by ambushes and sudden attacks.

The Celtiberians, a people born of the merging of Celts and Iberians, occupied the central and northern territories of the Iberian peninsula.

The Lusitani, a people whose culture was similar to that of the Celtiberians, lived in what is modern Portugal and a portion of the inland highlands of modern Spain.

the Senate of the great threat represented by Carthage, a city still far too rich and, above all, too close. Cato showed the Senate a handful of beautiful figs, and reminded them that they had been grown only three days away from Rome. Therefore, when the opportunity presented itself, Rome lost no time in starting the Third—and last—Punic War in 149 B.C. The Kingdom of Numidia, a Roman client state, complained of Carthaginian provocation. Rome accused Carthage of having broken the peace agreements. The great Punic city was put under siege and finally destroyed in 146 B.C. Rome celebrated the event in great triumph; the terrible adversary had been vanquished and its fertile lands and flourishing commerce had been made Rome's own.

The Spanish insurrection

Another of the matters still to be resolved for consolidation of the West was Spain, where, from 154 B.C. on, the Lusitani and the Celtiberians were in revolt. The Lusitani, under the able leadership of Viriathus, were tamed only in 139 B.C. after their leader was treacherously assassinated. The Celtiberians were also subjugated, although Numantia continued to defy the Romans until 133 B.C., when Scipio Aemilianus captured the city and razed it to the ground. At this point, Rome dominated the four great peninsulas of the Mediterranean (Italy, Spain, Greece, and Asia Minor), and the Balkans, as well as the northern coast of Africa. Other countries, such as

Numidia, Egypt, and Syria, which were not actually politically subject, could also consider themselves ruled by Rome.

Provinces and "provincials"

By the late second century B.C., Rome had created ten provinces in an immense territory outside of the Italian peninsula. Each province was governed by praetors (governors), who held full power. Many officials depended on them, including a quaestor for financial administration, *legati* (lieutenants) for military administration, and a host of "office workers" who handled the everyday business of government. Everywhere, the *lex provinciae*, or provincial charter, was adapted to the customs and uses of the various countries, but the Romans were intransigent on one point: They did not acknowledge any equality of rights between themselves and the conquered peoples, and being a Roman citizen, as opposed to a subject, was a great honor. The Italian populations, which were not incorporated as a province but were united with Rome, fought at length to attain the right to Roman citizenship.

Roman religion was traditionally public; it represented the state and one of its tasks was to reinforce citizens' loyalty to Rome. Above: The Temple of Vesta in the Forum Boarium (late second century B.C.)

Two-faced Janus was the god of beginnings and was consulted at the start of any activity.

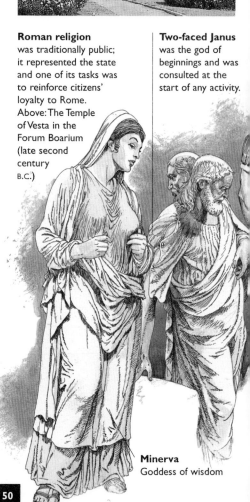

Minerva Goddess of wisdom

Mars
God of war

Jupiter
King of the gods

Juno
Queen of the gods

Neptune
God of the sea

Diana
Goddess of the moon and hunting.

Apollo
God of the sun and the arts

Venus
Goddess of love and the arts

THE ROMAN OLYMPUS
The ranks of the many Greek and Etruscan divinities that had been assimilated into Roman religion swelled with the conquest of Magna Graecia. They were later joined by Oriental deities, such as the Asian Cybele and the Egyptian Isis and Serapis.

51

TOWARD EMPIRE

Following the extraordinary military conquests of the second century B.C., Roman society underwent a great transformation. Contrasting social interests, personal ambition, and the aspirations of the subject peoples brought the republic to the brink of crisis.

Changes in society

The conquest of the Mediterranean and the East in the second century B.C. was accompanied by profound changes in Roman society; decadence and poverty grew as the Roman and Italian farmers lost their land, land holdings were combined and controlled by the rich, and great numbers of slaves were exploited for agricultural production.

During their long stints in the army, farmers were unable to cultivate the land. In order to support their families they contracted debts they were unable to pay and were then forced to transfer ownership of their farms to their creditors, abandon the land, and move to the cities—mainly to Rome—in search of new occupations. They could not even profit by the distribution of the public

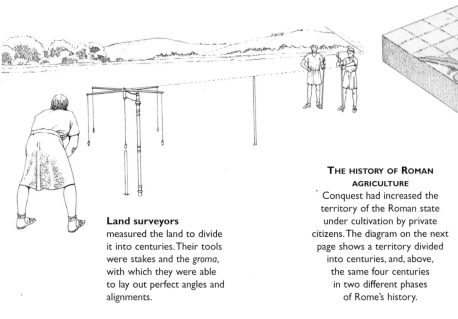

Land surveyors
measured the land to divide it into centuries. Their tools were stakes and the *groma*, with which they were able to lay out perfect angles and alignments.

THE HISTORY OF ROMAN AGRICULTURE
Conquest had increased the territory of the Roman state under cultivation by private citizens. The diagram on the next page shows a territory divided into centuries, and, above, the same four centuries in two different phases of Rome's history.

lands, since they were assigned for long rental periods. Moreover, the parcels were so large and costly that they completely excluded the small farmers. In the meantime, the conquests of foreign lands had brought immense fortunes to Rome. The most powerful members of the senatorial class, who secured a good part of this wealth for themselves, bought up small farms and thus increased their holdings. The ancient Roman farmer as small landowner was on the way out, and in his place emerged the great estate owner, who had abundant inexpensive labor available—the slaves, who were prisoners of

The century
was a square or rectangular parcel of land measuring 200 jugers (about 765 yards [700 m] per side) that had perpendicular roads and canals on either side.

Small allotments
Before the second century B.C., each century was divided up among 20 farmers. The different allotments are visible within the borders of the centuries.

The great estates
Each *latifundium* (estate), from the second century B.C. on, was made up of four or more centuries. The villa stood at the center of the cultivated land.

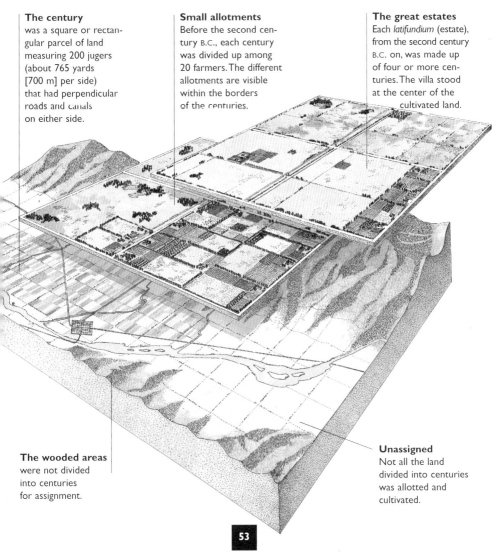

The wooded areas
were not divided into centuries for assignment.

Unassigned
Not all the land divided into centuries was allotted and cultivated.

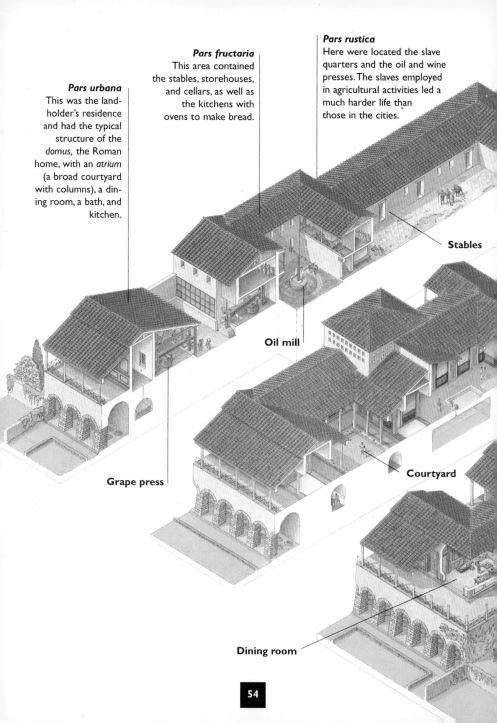

Pars urbana
This was the land-holder's residence and had the typical structure of the *domus,* the Roman home, with an *atrium* (a broad courtyard with columns), a dining room, a bath, and kitchen.

Pars fructaria
This area contained the stables, storehouses, and cellars, as well as the kitchens with ovens to make bread.

Pars rustica
Here were located the slave quarters and the oil and wine presses. The slaves employed in agricultural activities led a much harder life than those in the cities.

Stables

Oil mill

Grape press

Courtyard

Dining room

war. Rome's new dominion included immense territories in which agriculture flourished, and this caused great changes in the Italian economy. For example, local production of wheat became unnecessary.

Enormous wealth, immense opportunity, and epic conflicts

The provinces were rich in mineral resources and raw materials. They also represented vast markets for Rome's finished products. For the Romans, wealth had always been synonymous with possession of land. The members of the nobility, above all, began to amass properties and slaves. The 500 *jugers* (units of land) set as the land possession limit by the Liciniae Sextiae laws in the fourth century B.C. were no longer a valid reference. After the war with Hannibal, the aristocratic order pulled in their oars and access to the

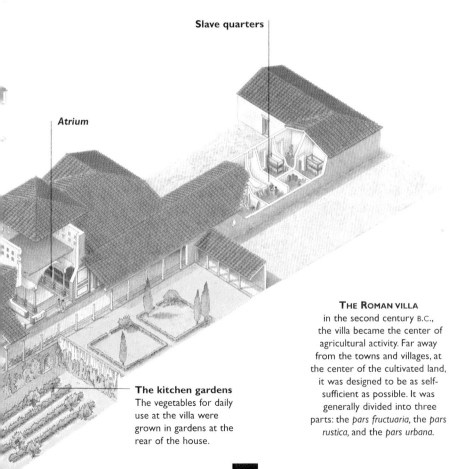

Slave quarters

Atrium

The kitchen gardens
The vegetables for daily use at the villa were grown in gardens at the rear of the house.

THE ROMAN VILLA
in the second century B.C., the villa became the center of agricultural activity. Far away from the towns and villages, at the center of the cultivated land, it was designed to be as self-sufficient as possible. It was generally divided into three parts: the *pars fructuaria*, the *pars rustica*, and the *pars urbana*.

consulships again became the privilege of a select few, the members of about 25 families. At the same time, however, some of the aristocrats took positions that differed with the ideas and interests of their order.

A second order began to gain power: the equestrian order of the *equites*, made up of people who had recently become rich. They prospered, mostly due to state contracts: provisioning the army, public works construction and maintenance, collecting levies and taxes, and mining. Other *equites* were moneylenders, bankers, and wealthy merchants.

During this time, Rome also acquired a sizable class of craftsmen, many of whom were freedmen, whose number, similar to that of the slaves, had increased from the Second Punic War on. The major craft activities were textiles and those of cobblers, potters, blacksmiths, ironsmiths, and porters. Due to the impoverishment of the farmers and the lack of new colonies, large numbers of unemployed farmers came to Rome and lived on donations and occasional jobs, offering their services to whatever politician would support them. A large number of people became aware of their problems and wanted to improve their lives. Some of the aristocrats fighting for power decided to organize these groups in their own favor.

The slaves

Naturally, no social class was worse off than the slaves. Their numbers had grown due to the enslavement of pris-

Literature flourishes Although considered superfluous in the past, literature flourished in the Hellenistic period. The greatest writers of this time were Terence, Accius, Pacuvius, Lucilius, and Ennius.

The scholarly slave Born in Tarentum and captured by the Romans during the war against his city, Livius Andronicus became the slave of Livius Salinator, a patrician who so appreciated his talents that he set him free. This slave became one of the greatest authors of Roman tragedies.

Masters and
familiares
At the top of the
social pyramid was
the estate holder
with his family.

The guardians
Management of the
slaves was entrusted
to a head guardian
who commanded
other overseers.

The overseers
were in the service
of the head guardian.
Their task was to
ensure that the
slaves obeyed
the orders they
were given.

Groups of slaves
were divided up
to ensure better
control by their
overseers.

Day workers
were sometimes
hired from nearby
fields to meet
seasonal demands
for labor.

THE ART OF SPEAKING
Beginning during the political struggles of the late second century B.C., marked by great historical events, the development of political ideas, and strong personalities, the time was ripe for oratory.

S.P.Q.R.
Senatus Populus Que Romanus: "The Senate and the People of Rome" was the emblem of the Roman state.

Oratory
During these years, the podiums of the Senate and the tribunals were the site of many disputes among the most eloquent personalities of the period. Literary works such as Cicero's *Brutus* and *De oratore* made the art of speaking a true academic discipline.

. S.P.Q.

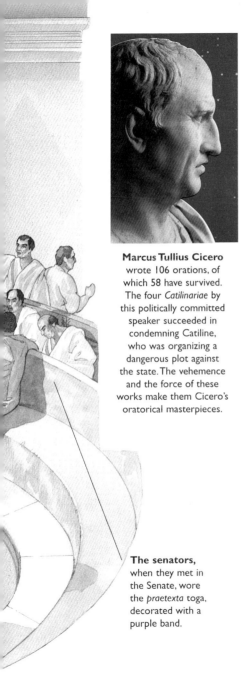

Marcus Tullius Cicero
wrote 106 orations, of
which 58 have survived.
The four *Catilinariae* by
this politically committed
speaker succeeded in
condemning Catiline,
who was organizing a
dangerous plot against
the state. The vehemence
and the force of these
works make them Cicero's
oratorical masterpieces.

The senators,
when they met in
the Senate, wore
the *praetexta* toga,
decorated with a
purple band.

oners of war, the birth of children of slaves, and the many slaves bought on the eastern slave markets on the island of Delos. It is said that more than 10,000 slaves a day were sold, most of them destined for Italy. The slaves employed as field hands were subjected to merciless exploitation and were under strict control and surveillance. Those in the cities enjoyed better conditions, but those engaged in herding were in the best condition for staging an armed revolt. Serious conflicts also simmered among the Romans and their Italian allies. Most of the allies lived in the same miserable conditions as the Roman farmers. Even the *élite* classes among the allies suffered discrimination and privation at the hands of Roman citizens.

The allies and the provincials

Other conflicts began in the provinces, between the Romans and the local populations. In the wars of conquest in Spain, Africa, Macedonia, Greece, and Asia Minor, the people had suffered a great deal. Following Roman conquest, the governors from the senatorial aristocracy and the publicans (newly wealthy people of the equestrian order) were brutal and rapacious. These strong differentiations within Roman society, the different aspirations of the two dominant groups, the great discontent among farmers driven off their lands, the masses of city-dwellers with no permanent occupation, and the tensions between Romans and allies and between Romans and provincials created a state of growing political and institutional crisis. It soon became clear that the various political and economic reforms that were proposed would be unable to resolve these problems and conflicts of interests. There thus began a long period, about 100 years, of escalating violence, revolts, and civil wars that threatened the very foundations of the republican institutions.

The Gracchi

Tiberious and Gaius Gracchus, nobles by birth, became the defenders of the people. The first to appear on the political scene was Tiberius, who in 133 B.C., presented an agrarian law by which all those who possessed more than 500 *jugers* (about 310 acres [125 ha]) of public land would have to return the excess part to the state. The land thus recovered would have been distributed to

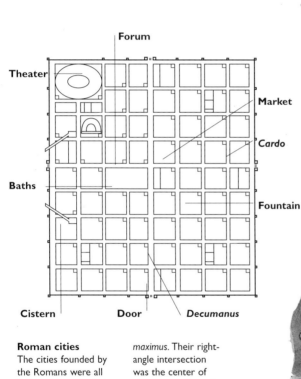

Roman cities
The cities founded by the Romans were all built on a standard plan. Two perfectly straight thoroughfares were laid out: the *cardo maximus* and the *decumanus* *maximus*. Their right-angle intersection was the center of the city, usually at the forum. All around were city blocks on a uniform square plan.

THE STREETS OF ROME
In building their new cities, the Romans imported the grid layout with wide streets, but in Rome itself the natural development of the city made it impossible to follow the urban plan.

The insulae
were low-cost housing units on a high-rise plan. On the ground floors were taverns and shops.

The *vici*
Most of the streets in Rome were *vici*: narrow, dirty alleys, usually without sidewalks.

Construction density
determined the existence of passages and blind alleys.

the poorer citizens in small lots of 30 *jugers* (about 18.5 acres [7.5 ha]) each. This plan went against the interests of the senators, the majority of whom were estate owners, and met with strong opposition. Despite everything, Tiberius was such an able politician that he managed to have the law passed, but he paid dearly for his victory; the Senate had him assassinated and his law was put aside. Ten years later, Tiberius's plan was again brought up by his brother Gaius. During his term as tribune of the plebs, in 123–122 B.C., he launched a far-reaching series of reforms. He ensured support from the publicans of the equestrian order by granting them,

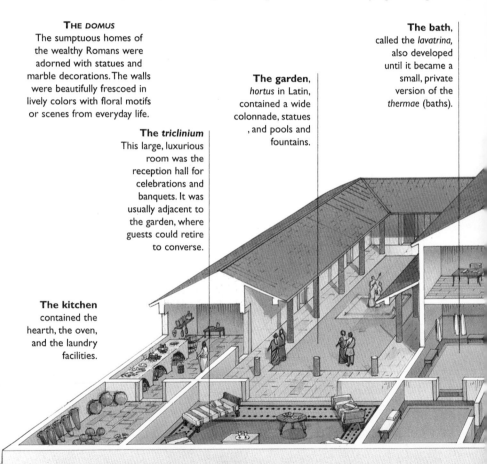

THE DOMUS
The sumptuous homes of the wealthy Romans were adorned with statues and marble decorations. The walls were beautifully frescoed in lively colors with floral motifs or scenes from everyday life.

The triclinium
This large, luxurious room was the reception hall for celebrations and banquets. It was usually adjacent to the garden, where guests could retire to converse.

The garden, *hortus* in Latin, contained a wide colonnade, statues , and pools and fountains.

The bath, called the *lavatrina*, also developed until it became a small, private version of the *thermae* (baths).

The kitchen contained the hearth, the oven, and the laundry facilities.

among other benefits, the right to pass judgment on abuses of power by the senators. This accelerated the politicization of the equestrian order, and its problems with the senators. Gaius also began distributing grain at a low cost to the people of Rome. Other administrative measures of his were also successful, but he met with failure when he

attempted to revive Tiberius's agrarian reform, and to obtain citizenship for the Latins and voting rights for the allies in the popular assembly. The reaction of the senatorial order to his proposals was harsh, and in 121 B.C., Gaius Gracchus died a violent death. With the Gracchi out of the way, the interests of the senators again prevailed; the party

The *tablinium* was the dining room on the side of the house opposite the entrance.

The central *atrium* This space contained the *impluvium*, a large pool in which rainwater collected.

The bedrooms The *cubicola*, the bedrooms, extended along the sides of the *atrium*.

Heating Hot air was channeled through spaces under the mosaic floors to heat the *domus*.

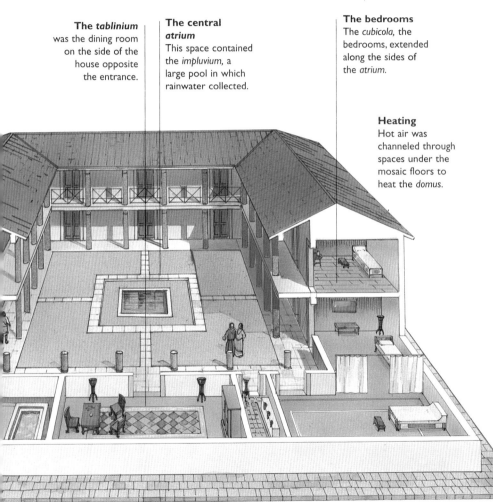

of the aristocrats had defeated the popular party but had not solved any of the basic problems plaguing Rome.

A new man in power

This time it was an event outside of Rome that caused an important political turn. In the second century B.C., in Africa (more precisely in the allied kingdom of Numidia), the usurper Jugurtha was greatly damaging the interests of Roman businessmen and merchants. Those members of the equestrian order whose interests were most directly affected opposed the ineffective political reaction of the Senate, and in 107 B.C. elected a new man as consul: the energetic Gaius Marius. With no illustrious ancestors,

BATTLE POSITIONS
At the order to fight, the legion took up positions in three echelons.

The cavalry
defended the wings of the legion to prevent it from being surrounded.

The line
Each line consisted of 10 maniples. Spaces were left to permit the passage of the *velites*, light-armed infantry who launched stones and other projectiles, then immediately retreated back through the lines.

but intelligent and enterprising, Marius captured Jugurtha in 105 B.C. In going to war, Gaius Marius had to solve a new problem that had to do with Rome's basic tool of expansion and conquest: the army.

Until that time, the army had been enlisted on the basis of the census, among those who could afford the needed equipment. With the farm-ers' social crisis and the economic slump, the basis for conscription no longer existed. Marius thus exploit-ed the growing masses of those with-out property who lived in Rome. He called for volunteers, making no dis-tinctions as to census class. Marius's army was thus made up of both con-scripts and volunteers. This required a change in the Romans' way of

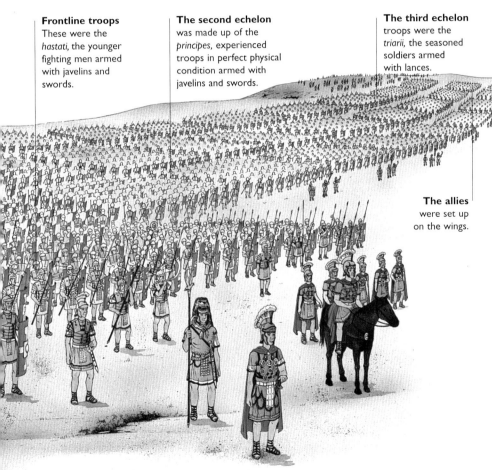

Frontline troops
These were the *hastati*, the younger fighting men armed with javelins and swords.

The second echelon
was made up of the *principes*, experienced troops in perfect physical condition armed with javelins and swords.

The third echelon
troops were the *triarii*, the seasoned soldiers armed with lances.

The allies
were set up on the wings.

Head
from the tomb of Valerii (Vatican Museums), late second century B.C. Although the artists that actually made the works were mostly Greek, the portrait was representative of Roman custom and the patrician outlook.

Sulla
as represented in a portrait from 80–75 B.C., in Venice's Museo Archeologico. Sulla's reforms deprived the tribunes of the plebs of almost all their powers, increased the number of senators, and established inflexible rules to prevent generals from using force against Rome.

Ancestors
Since the earliest times, the Roman patricians displayed the busts of their ancestors in their homes, to celebrate the illustrious past of their families and to express their pride in their noble houses. Left: *Patrician with Busts of Ancestors* (early first century A.D.). Palazzo dei Conservatori, Rome.

thinking about the army and of its very nature. The military vocation became less an expression of the Roman population and more linked to personal interest and loyalty to one's commander. These new features were to prove decisive in domestic matters in the Rome of the first century B.C.

The civil war
In the first century B.C., there began a period of serious contrasts. First, the Italian allies, who for years had demanded Roman citizenship in vain, revolted and fought vigorously until they were granted the right they had long sought. This matter had barely been settled when Rome became involved in civil war. Its protagonists

were Marius, at the head of the popular party, and Sulla, the defender of the Senate and the aristocrats. Both wanted to conduct the war against Mithradates, king of Pontus (a region of Asia Minor that was still independent), but command was assigned to Sulla. Marius thus plotted to replace his rival at any cost, and for three years Rome was devastated by internal struggles, executions, and massacres by various supporters of the two factions. First Sulla had a number of members of the popular party put to death, forcing Marius to flee Rome. Then Marius's army sacked Rome and slaughtered entire families. Sulla eventually won and as dictator instituted reforms that reinforced the power of the aristocrats. However, the inability of the dominant order to understand the needs of society created a situation of instability. Two new commanders now appeared on the scene and attempted to restore order.

Pompey and Caesar

Between 73 and 71 B.C., Marcus Licinius Crassus put down the revolt of the slaves led by Spartacus, while from 76 to 72 B.C. Gnaeus Pompeius thwarted a revolt in Spain. In 70 B.C., a few years after Sulla's retirement from the political scene, Pompeius (now called Pompey the Great) and Crassus were elected consuls. They should not have been able to attain the post because they did not have the qualifications called for by the constitution, but their armies were camped outside the walls of Rome, ready to move at the slightest sign, and the Senate had

Young woman
Elaborate hairstyles exalted the beauty of Rome's young women. Left: A portrait from the first century A.D. in Rome's Musei Capitolini.

Head of patrician
Portraits, especially those of the republican age, are characterized by great realism that emphasizes the real features of the face, even when these were less than perfect or even unpleasant. The Romans demanded this sort of realism, since they considered themselves strong and wanted to communicate this image. Right: Head of a patrician (first century B.C.). Museo Torlonia, Rome.

little choice in the matter. At first it seemed that the two could govern together in full accord, and, in fact, one of their first actions was to abolish Sulla's reforms. Then conflicts arose between them, and the Senate, in order to avoid a new civil war, sent Pompey to put an end to the actions of the pirates in the Mediterranean and then against Mithradates, who was threatening Rome's Asian provinces. While Pompey was fighting (and winning) everywhere, Crassus remained in Rome where, together with the young aristocrat Gaius Julius Caesar, he led the popular party in opposition to two eminent personalities who headed the

Matrons
wore the *stola*, a long dress with many folds, belted at the waist. It was worn over a tunic.

Jewels
Earrings, diadems, necklaces, and rings brightened women's apparel with the sparkle of gold, silver, and such precious stones as sapphires, garnets, and rubies.

party of the aristocrats: Marcus Porcius Cato and Marcus Tullius Cicero.

The first triumvirate

Julius Caesar was able and intelligent and out to weaken the authority of the Senate, but in order to do so he needed prestigious allies. He thus played on the discontent of Pompey, who upon his triumphant return from the East was very disturbed by the Senate's refusal to grant the land promised to his veterans. Caesar also enlisted the aid of Crassus, who possessed immense wealth and wielded considerable influence with the *equites*. Thus, in 60 B.C., the first triumvirate was formed. It was a secret agreement that

The gladiators
were slaves who fought in the circuses. They led a hard life and were subjected to arduous training.

The tunic
Roman aristocrats wore the toga over the tunic, the basic element of their wardrobes. With time, the comfortable and practical tunic became the daily outfit of the men and the toga was worn only on certain political and social occasions.

Thumbs down
The people decided the fate of a defeated gladiator. By raising their thumbs they spared his life; a thumbs down decreed his death.

GLADIATOR CONTESTS
Romans were particularly fond of bloody spectacles and ferocious combat.

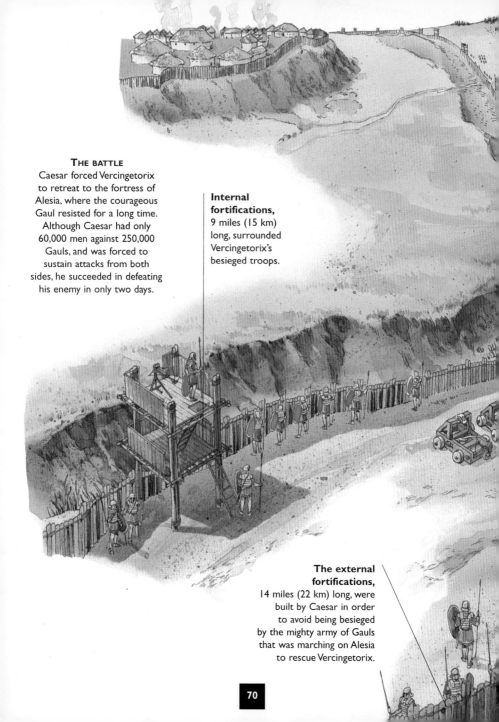

The battle

Caesar forced Vercingetorix to retreat to the fortress of Alesia, where the courageous Gaul resisted for a long time. Although Caesar had only 60,000 men against 250,000 Gauls, and was forced to sustain attacks from both sides, he succeeded in defeating his enemy in only two days.

Internal fortifications, 9 miles (15 km) long, surrounded Vercingetorix's besieged troops.

The external fortifications, 14 miles (22 km) long, were built by Caesar in order to avoid being besieged by the mighty army of Gauls that was marching on Alesia to rescue Vercingetorix.

in practice was an exceptional coalition of different types of power. Crassus represented economic force; Pompey, military might; and Caesar, the party of the democrats—the people. Thanks to this alliance, Caesar was elected consul in 59 B.C. He took the policies of the Gracchi and managed to force the Senate to pass an important agrarian law that called for distribution of the public land to Pompey's veterans and to the poorest citizens. At the end of his term as consul, he became governor of Cisalpine Gaul and of Illyria (the Dalmatian peninsula) for a five-year period. Caesar's consulship was of historic importance because it marked the definite eclipse of the power of the Senate and the passage from the republic to the monarchy.

First of all, Caesar had obtained a military command for five years, and this unprecedented case in the history of Rome provided him with the foundation on which he later built his power. Then, in an astute political maneuver, he succeeded in eliminating both Cicero and Cato, the intelligent and authoritative heads of the Senate, from the political scene. This was the scenario Caesar left behind when he departed for his victorious campaigns in Gaul.

The conquest of Gaul
Independent Gaul, which extended from the Pyrenees to the Rhine, was in Caesar's time divided into three parts: central Gaul (from the Garonne to the Seine), northeastern Gaul (from the Seine to the Rhine), and western Gaul.

Certain nomadic populations were fighting among themselves in these territories, and Caesar took advantage of the situation to conquer the entire region between 58 and 56 B.C. The Gauls, who before the Roman conquest had been divided into many mutually hostile tribes, formed a coalition and in 52 B.C., led by Vercingetorix, rose up against Rome. It was a year of hard-fought battles, but Caesar, after having defeated Vercingetorix at Alesia, managed to pacify all of Gaul and to make it, in 52 B.C., a Roman province.

Caesar and Pompey

In the meantime, there were conflicts in Rome between the people and the Senate, and Caesar faced a serious threat: Pompey, who was elected sole consul with full powers in 51 B.C., had slowly won over the Senate and had begun a movement opposing Caesar. Thus, in 49 B.C., Caesar decided to resolve matters by marching on Rome with his armed troops and forcing Pompey and the Senate to flee the city. Pompey died in Alexandria, Egypt, where Caesar also had landed in order to settle the fight for succession between Ptolemy and his sister Cleopatra. Pompey's followers continued to fight against Caesar but were defeated many times and finally routed at Munda in 45 B.C.

Caesar's "princedom"

Caesar became the sole and absolute master of the republic. In 49 B.C., while he was in Spain, he was appointed dictator with the task of reorganizing the

JULIUS CAESAR
promoted an agrarian reform and often distributed grain and money to the poor of Rome. His economic and civil reforms were many and he increased the number of magistracies so as to dilute their power.

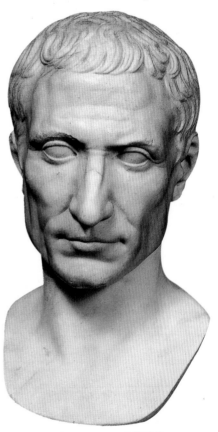

Gaius Julius Caesar
Free Roman citizens had three names: the given name, the *praenomen*; their family name, *gens*, called the *nomen*; and the *cognomen*. Gaius Julius Caesar was of the gens *Julia*, hence the *nomen* Julius. Gaius was his *praenomen*, and Caesar his *cognomen*. In certain cases, as in Africanus for Scipio and Censor for Cato, a second *cognomen* was added.

state, and in 46 B.C. he was again appointed dictator, this time for ten years. In practice, Rome had for some time been looking to Caesar as its only hope of salvation, and therefore, in 44 B.C., he was appointed dictator for life. This meant that all the powers of the state centered on him, yet he refused to accept the formal title of king that had been offered to him. He dreamed of a universal monarchy similar to that of the great Macedonian leader Alexander the Great, who in the fourth century B.C. had created an empire that reached from Greece to the borders of India. He began by granting Roman citizenship to the inhabitants of Cisalpine Gaul (modern northern Italy) and to some provinces. But Caesar was assassinated on March 15, 44 B.C. While his death put an end to his plans, it also heralded new and serious threats for the Roman state.

Caesar's conquests
During his reign, Caesar added Gaul (modern France, Belgium, and the Netherlands) to Rome's already vast territory.

The Roman calendar
Caesar reformed the calendar; it was no longer based on the lunar year (355 days) but on the 365-day solar year. He also invented leap years.

Roman coins
The basic monetary unit in the fourth century B.C. was the bronze *as*. The silver *denarius*, coined in the third century, was the most valued republican coin, with a value of 10 *asses*. Another fraction of the *denarius* was the *sesterce*, worth 2.5

asses. The gold *aureus* was worth 25 *denarii*. Caesar's broad reform of the monetary system, designed to better meet the needs of the new state, was not implemented before his death. Above: A coin minted with the effigy of Julius Caesar.

Calends, ides,* and *nones
Each month had three special days corresponding to the phases of the moon. The first day of the month, at the new moon, was the *calends;*

the seventh, at the first quarter, was the *nones;* the fifteenth, at the full moon, was the *ides.* Caesar was assassinated on the *ides* of March, 44 B.C.

ALEXANDRIA, EGYPT
Founded by Alexander the Great in
332 B.C., Alexandria soon became
one of the most important cities
in the ancient world. This famous
cultural and economic center
was home to celebrated schools of
literature, art, and philosophy.

The Lighthouse
was one of the Seven
Wonders of the ancient
world. It stood on the
peninsula on the side of
the city's two ports.

A spectacular city
Alexandria was large
and opulent and many
of its buildings were
among the most
extraordinary of
the period.

**The colonnaded
portico of the
Museum**
The Great Museum was
built to host a group of
scholars. It became the
most important center
of Hellenistic culture.

Anthony vs. Octavian

Caesar's death threw Rome into civil war. This time, the contenders were Anthony, consul that year, and Octavian, Caesar's adopted son. In the beginning, the two made an agreement, together with Anthony's official, Lepidus. It was called the Second Triumvirate, a five-year magistracy. Octavian and Anthony chased Caesar's assassins to Greece, and defeated them at Philippi in 42 B.C. After managing to deprive Lepidus of his title as triumvir, Anthony gained full power over the East, while to Octavian went the West. Anthony went to Egypt; he had fallen in love with Cleopatra, and after having repudiated his wife Octavia (Octavian's sister), married her. He then gave Cleopatra the gift of Egypt and certain of the Syrian regions under Roman rule. Rome's reaction was immediate. Octavian took the occasion to eliminate his rival and met him in battle at Actium, off western Greece, in 31 B.C. Octavian's more manageable ships were sūperior to those of Anthony. Anthony fled with Cleopatra, leaving the Egyptian fleet leaderless and at the mercy of the Romans, who proceeded to almost completely destroy it. In 30 B.C., Octavian succeeded in entering Alexandria and Anthony, seeing that all was lost, committed suicide. Cleopatra followed his example, by provoking the bite of an asp. In the fall of 29 B.C., Octavian returned to Rome where his victory celebration lasted three days. The era of the republic was ended forever.

A cosmpolitan city
Although Alexandria preserved many characteristics of Egyptian civilization, its culture was Greek, as its founder wanted. Over time, it filled up with people of every race and culture, who worked together to make this city an incredibly cosmopolitan center, a true universal city in the best Hellenistic tradition.

THE ROMAN EMPIRE

Octavian inaugurated a personal form of government called the principate. It marked the beginning of a period of splendor that lasted until the second century A.D. The empire became a single political and cultural entity that reached its maximum expansion under Trajan.

The political struggle in Rome gradually increased in intensity from the second century B.C. on. Conflicts evolved into violent skirmishes and finally into civil wars. It had become all too apparent how difficult it was to govern the vast territories Rome had acquired if power was not strongly centralized. The seemingly interminable succession of civil wars eventually created a consuming desire for peace in the Roman people.

The principate

When he returned to Rome in 29 B.C., victorious over Anthony, Octavian was the sole lord of the city. He gradually took on full powers without openly declaring himself king. The title of *imperator* (commander-in-chief of the army), that of *Augustus* ("he who provides for the good of the citizens"), and those of *pontifex maximus* (greatest pontiff), and *pater patriae* (father of the country) all increased

Augustus as
pontifex maximus
The emperor is shown with the symbols of his maximum religious authority. This type of celebrative statue is typical of the official Roman art of the time, since its aim was to convey the glory of Rome in all its various aspects.

The *horologium Augusti*,
the solar clock built by Augustus in the Campus Martius, consisted of a gigantic obelisk, brought to Rome from Egypt. It projected its shadow on a broad paved dial.

What time is it?
The pavement was marked with bronze letters and lines from which the time could be calculated based on the position of the shadow on the ground.

The *Ara Pacis*
is the monument ordered raised by the Senate in honor of Augustus. Richly decorated with images celebrating the grandeur of Rome and Augustus's peace, the altar reflected the new, extraordinary world created by the emperor.

THE PAX AUGUSTA
was Augustus's masterpiece. There was peace everywhere. This did not mean the cessation of military activity, which was still considered necessary to guarantee defense and consolidate the empire, but rather coexistence of the various peoples and their unification under Roman rule.

A yearly appointment
On September 23, Augustus's birthday, the shadow of the obelisk touched the *Ara Pacis*.

CITY MANAGEMENT
Rome was large and crowded, divided into 14 districts, and entrusted to 3 prefects, each of them with specific responsibilities.

Supplies
Provision of grain and all other supplies to Rome was coordinated by the *praefectus annonae* (prefect of grain supply).

Taxation
was based on the *fiscus* and the *aerarium*. The *fiscus* collected taxes from the imperial provinces, used for upkeep of the army. The *aerarium* collected taxes from the senatorial provinces and paid expenses inherent to civil administration.

his authority. Augustus's principate (from *princeps,* meaning "first citizen") lasted for more than 40 years and marked a turning point in the history of Rome, both in terms of internal political stability and the peace he brought to the empire as a whole. Augustus's greatest talent lay in governing Rome as a monarch and succeeding in appearing, to the eyes of the Senate and the Roman people, a loyal servant of the state and its institutions. He was highly respectful toward the Senate, even though he drastically reduced its power. He distributed the highest state posts in part to the senators and in part to the *equites.* Augustus, and his successors after him, promoted the entry into the Senate of new men selected to participate in the managerial elite based

The urban cohorts were 3 in number, for a total of about 3,000 men. They were commanded by the *praefectus urbi* (prefect of the city) and were in charge of keeping order up to 100 miles (161 km) from the capital.

The night watch in Rome was entrusted to 7,000 men divided into 7 cohorts, superintended by the *praefectus vigilum*. These men were also firefighters.

solely on their outstanding abilities.

The choice made on merit and not merely on the basis of noble birth was in part dictated by the need to add to the Senate, which had become increasingly insular and which would have decreased in number if measures had not been taken to correct the situation. As part of his effort to ensure the smooth operation of the state, Augustus also set out to reorganize Rome's vase empire. Italy was divided into 11 regions, each governed by a magistrate; the provinces were of two types: senatorial and imperial. The former were the more peaceful regions in which the presence of the army was not needed.

The governing proconsuls had no military powers. The imperial provinces were more turbulent and insecure and required troops with expert commanders. They were thus governed directly by the emperor through trusted legates. The most important posts in public adminstration were nevertheless reserved for the members of the highest social orders, the senators and the *equites*. Adminstration of the single urban communities was entrusted to the local élites, who formed the decurionate. Augustus created a permanent professional army of 350,000 to 400,000 soldiers. Military service became a career by choice, and the period of enlistment was lengthy. Nine praetorian cohorts were created to provide Augustus with a personal guard.

Construction
While they were being built, the great Roman arches were supported by wooden scaffolding that was taken down when work was completed.

THE ART OF BUILDING
The Romans were extraordinary builders, and all their architecture embodies three fundamental principles: strength, function, and beauty.

The aqueducts
The Romans never skimped on either costs or labor to provide fresh water to the cities. Water was channeled from distant springs through tunnels cut into mountains and over colossal arches across the countryside.

Cement
The discovery of a wet mixture of stone, lime, and sand, which makes cement, was important for Roman architecture, since it added strength to the buildings.

The cupola
In the Imperial Age, the vault became an essential element of architecture, thanks to cement, which replaced stone and brick and made it possible to raise huge vaulted domes. Right: The interior of the Pantheon in Rome.

THE THEATER OF MARCELLUS
was located in the Campus
Martius between the Capitoline
and the Tiber. Begun by Caesar, it
was completed in A.D. 13 by
Augustus, who dedicated it to the
memory of his nephew Marcellus
who had died ten years earlier.

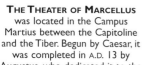

The mask
covered the entire
face of the actor
and incorporated
a funnel-shaped
mouthpiece that
aided in projecting
the actor's voice.
Different masks
represented the
characters in
various moods.

The *scaena*
was 121 feet (37 m)
wide and was adorned
with enormous columns
and statues.

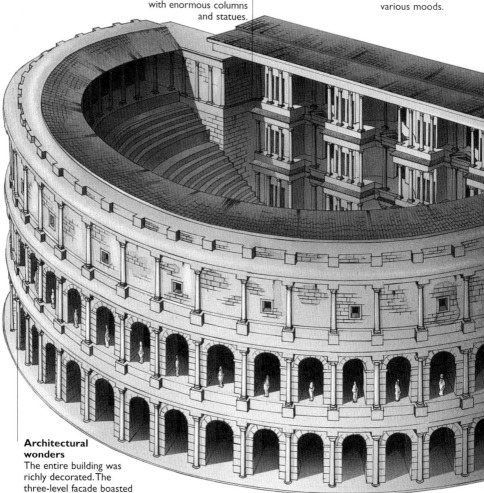

**Architectural
wonders**
The entire building was
richly decorated. The
three-level facade boasted
41 arches framed by
semicolumns.

Titus Maccius Plautus, born in about 250 B.C., was one of the greatest Latin comedy writers. Many of his works were based on misunderstandings or mistaken identity, and showed a humorous style of comedy. Above: Strolling players in a mosaic from Pompeii.

The actors were called *histriones*.

The building Splendid and elegant, the theater was almost 426 feet (130 m) in diameter and more than 105 feet (32 m) high, with a capacity of 20,000 spectators.

Empire

The Roman Empire was immense. It extended from West to East, and the population of the many very different regions that composed it is estimated by historians at between 50 and 80 million. Augustus reorganized this enormous territory and kept it solidly united thanks to the power of his army and to an extraordinarily efficient administrative organization based on cooperation between the subject peoples and the Romans. The provinces were Rome's great wealth. Unlike before, the vast conquered territories were no longer considered simply as places to be stripped of value and from which the powerful Roman senators could draw personal advantage. Augustus created an imperial monarchy, and the provinces were integrated into the social and economic system of the empire. The Roman model was successfully transmitted to the populations of the majority of the provinces.

There was general belief in the universal concept of empire, that expansion should continue and that the empire should extend until it reached its "natural," physically recognizable and defensible borders. For this reason, Augustus eliminated the areas of resistance within the empire, for example in Spain, and subjugated those few Alpine regions that were not yet under Rome's direct rule. After failing to conquer Germany, Augustus set the northern limits of the empire at the Rhine and Danube.

The economy under the principate

The long Golden Age of Rome began under Augustus. Peace, power, culutral splendor, and great economic growth were the keystones of the Augustun era and of the following two centuries of the principate.

Both the social system of orders and classes of the republican period and the economic system based on the absolute primacy of agriculture remained substantially unchanged in the passage from republic to principate. About 90 percent of the population of the empire was employed in agriculture. Only a few of the more than 1,000 cities of the empire had populations exceeding 10,000 to 15,000. Wealth came from the land, and the northern provinces of the

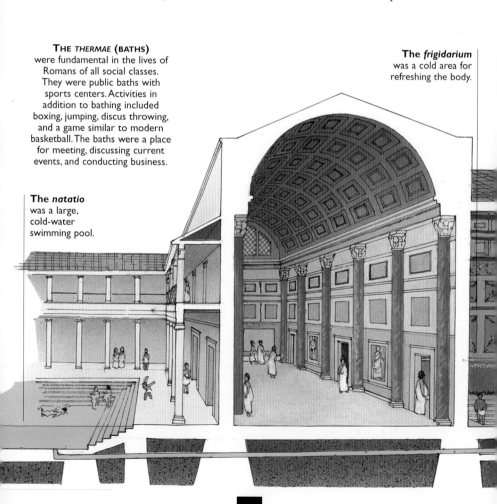

THE *THERMAE* (BATHS) were fundamental in the lives of Romans of all social classes. They were public baths with sports centers. Activities in addition to bathing included boxing, jumping, discus throwing, and a game similar to modern basketball. The baths were a place for meeting, discussing current events, and conducting business.

The *natatio* was a large, cold-water swimming pool.

The *frigidarium* was a cold area for refreshing the body.

empire achieved yields close to those of Egypt and other productive areas.

The division into social classes was very clear; the members of the upper classes (the senatorial and equestrian orders and the decurions of the imperial cities) numbered not more than 200,000, or about 1 percent of the population. The lower classes were made up of very different urban and

Frescoes decorated the public buildings and the homes of the wealthiest Romans.

Above: A detail of the late second-century B.C. decoration of the walls of the house of Livia in Rome.

The *tepidarium* The cooler area that followed the *calidarium*.

The *calidarium* was the heated portion of the *thermae,* for hot baths.

above all rural groups. Vital for the Roman economic system was the great number of slaves, despite the reduction of prisoners of war. In Italy, of about 7.5 million inhabitants, 3 million were slaves.

Augustus's Rome

Rome was transformed from controlling city to capital of the empire. It was splendid, but overcrowded. With about one million inhabitants, Rome had 37 gates, 7 bridges over the Tiber, 18 aqueducts, 400 temples, 147,000 homes, and 2,000 palaces. Thirty-one military roads started out from the forum. At the center of the city were the public offices and the forum. The hills—especially the Aventine and the Quirinal—had become the residential areas of the aristocrats and the rich, and Suburra and Velabrum were the districts where the majority of the ordinary people lived. The low-income housing had become islands, multistory buildings standing in a maze of narrow, foul-smelling alleyways. Rome had grown too fast, with no real plan. Serious intervention was called for to stabilize the expansion of the residential areas, modernize the public buildings, and improve communications among the various districts. Under Augustus, Rome became an immense construction site. It was commonly said that Augustus found a city of brick and left one of marble. He could not improve all of Rome's housing, but he did add unparalleled palaces, monuments, baths, and the-

THE FORUM OF AUGUSTUS, inaugurated in 2 B.C., was built on a vast area that was previously a residential district. The land was purchased by the emperor with the proceeds of his successful military campaigns.

The structure
The forum was rectangular in form and decorated with porticoes and colonnades. It faithfully copied the architectural model provided by Caesar's forum (46 B.C.), which also inspired the forums of Nerva (A.D. 97) and Vespasian (A.D. 75).

The Temple
of Mars Ultor, the avenger of Caesar's murder, was dedicated by Augustus in 42 B.C. prior to the Battle of Philippi.

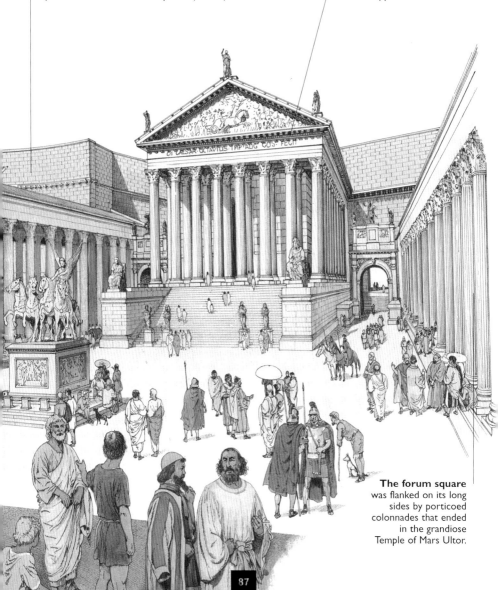

The forum square
was flanked on its long sides by porticoed colonnades that ended in the grandiose Temple of Mars Ultor.

THE FLAVIAN AMPHITHEATER, begun by Vespasian in A.D. 72, was ideal for great gladiator contests. It was called the Colosseum because of its proximity to a colossal statue of Nero.

A colossal structure, oval in form, 161 feet (49 m) high with a perimeter of 1,761 feet (537 m).

The flooring Sand (*arena* in Latin) was spread over a wooden base. The sandy floor absorbed the blood shed in the contests.

Elevators, driven by winches, carried the animals and gladiators up to the arena.

aters. He also gave the capital a new forum. Augustus's version of this open space surrounded by a colonnade was a grandiose 335 feet (102 m) per side. Augustus was also the grand patron of the culture of his times. Literature reached its highest level, thanks to the outstanding talents of Horace, Virgil, Ovid, and Livy. Figurative art produced beautiful, refined works, and philosophy blossomed in the many literary circles in which Romans met to converse and comment on events.

Imperial doings

Augustus died in A.D. 14. His reorganization had laid sound bases for the

Vespasian in the guise of military leader (portrait from A.D. 75). This is an example of official art that celebrated the grandeur of the emperor and of Rome through the representation of military symbols, conveying the idea of Rome's power (Museo delle Terme, Rome).

Underground Under the flooring were animal cages, rooms for the gladiators, and ramps that linked the different service levels.

empire, but it still needed improvement. A period of instability followed with Augustus' first four successors (Tiberius, Caligula, Claudius, and Nero), the so-called Julian-Claudian dynasty. The situation was, in fact, extremely complex, with contrasts. Besides the emperor there were three other major centers of power: the Senate, which refused to relinquish its authority; the praetorians, the emperor's personal guard, who became more and more powerful and influential; and the commanders of the army. Although the legions were scattered throughout the empire, they were attentive to political events in the capital. All this must be seen against the background of the people of Rome, the great masses of the poor and disinherited in search of a place to live and resources for survival. Augustus had succeeded in balancing off all these centers of power, but the personalities of the Julio-Claudian emperors were certainly not equal to that of their illustrious predecessor. Caligula, who succeeded Tiberius in A.D. 37, not only proved to be incapable of ruling but headed for outright tyranny. Thus the praetorian guard, in agreement with the senate, assassinated him in A.D. 41 and replaced him with Claudius, an old and mild man. At Claudius' death, Nero ascended the throne. At first he seemed willing to cooperate with the Senate, but, gradually, he turned to the people for support and instituted an antisenatorial policy. The serious conflicts that followed, together with the emperor's eccentricities, led to a great revolt. Both the praetorians and the troops of several provinces participated, causing Nero to commit suicide. The revolt continued after his death and became a struggle for power in which the members of the senatorial order, the praetorians, and the commanders of the other legions of the empire all took part. In the end, the commander of the eastern legions, Vespasian, won. He was the first "new Roman" of humble origins to achieve the status of *princeps*.

THE JEWISH UPRISINGS
The Jews were in revolt because of the oppression of Roman officials. Rome decided to end the rebellions by laying siege to Jerusalem. After five months of resistance, the city surrendered to Titus in A.D. 70.

The diaspora
The majority of the Jews were deported and dispersed, but Rabbi ben Zakkai succeeded in getting permission from his Roman captors to set up an academy in Jamnia (Jabneh), near the Judaean coast. Through this and other schools that were later set up, the Jews succeeded in keeping their religious traditions alive through the ages.

The Western Wall
Today, Jews still come to the Western or Wailing Wall, all that is left of the foundation of the Second Temple in Jerusalem.

The Temple of Jerusalem, the great sanctuary of the Jewish religion in the time of Solomon, contained the Ark of the Covenant and the Tablets of the Law (Ten Commandments) received by Moses on Mount Sinai. Titus completely destroyed both the temple and the city.

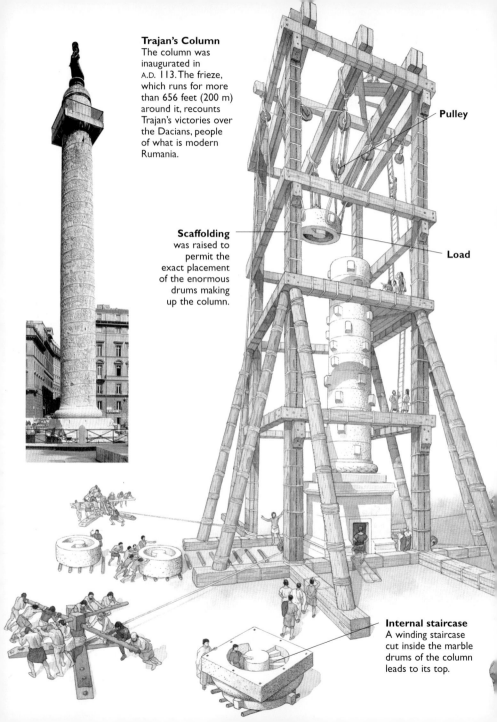

Trajan's Column
The column was inaugurated in A.D. 113. The frieze, which runs for more than 656 feet (200 m) around it, recounts Trajan's victories over the Dacians, people of what is modern Rumania.

Pulley

Scaffolding was raised to permit the exact placement of the enormous drums making up the column.

Load

Internal staircase
A winding staircase cut inside the marble drums of the column leads to its top.

Major changes

Vespasian reigned from A.D. 69 to 79. His first acts as emperor aimed at creating a solid foundation for his authority. With his laws, he officially and unequivocally concentrated in the emperor the powers of sovereign. This weakened the authority of the Senate and at the same time eliminated the army's interference. He was a talented administrator. The state coffers were empty following the wasteful spending of his predecessors and the devastation of the civil wars, but Vespasian succeeded in putting public finance in order through a series of strong measures. He granted Roman citizenship to all of Spain, with the aim of introducing many new citizens of this province into the Senate and therefore breaking up the interest groups that persisted around the old senatorial families. He charged his son Titus with putting down the Jewish revolt, and in A.D. 70 Titus destroyed Jerusalem. When he succeeded Vespasian in A.D. 79, he continued his father's policies and governed wisely. At his death in A.D. 81, his brother Domitian ascended the throne, but his cruel, despotic ways aroused such hatred in the Senate and the people that he fell victim to a conspiracy in A.D. 96. Domitian was the last of the hereditary emperors. The Senate elected the wise, moderate Nerva, who, in turn, instituted the system of succession by adoption, and named Marcus Ulpius Traianus as his heir.

MONUMENT BUILDING
By erecting a monument, in this case a great column, the emperor depicted the greatness of his exploits.

The army
A soldier of Trajan's army carries a bull to be sacrificed on the altar.

Winches
A team of workers use a horizontal winch to maneuver the hoist from the ground.

The sacrifice
Emperor Trajan offers a sacrifice to the gods. The votive offerings burn on the altar.

The bridge
In the background is seen the wooden bridge on stone pylons built over the Danube in A.D. 104.

Trajan: The first provincial emperor

Born in Spain, Trajan came to power in A.D. 98. He was the first "provincial" to head the empire, and as emperor he had few equals for intelligence and outlook. He was always extremely respectful to the Senate and continued Nerva's policy of support for the poorest families, gave a strong stimulus to both trade and industry, built up Rome through grandiose construction projects, drained the Pontine marshes, and extended the *Via Appia* as far as Brindisium. He was an extraordinary general, defeating both the Dacians and the Parthians, and stretching the empire to the maximum. He was a great emperor whose time was marked by a culture that permeated all sectors thanks to his strong sense of liberty and tolerance.

The rise of the provincials

Trajan had helped Rome to expand to the maximum as an empire. It was similar to Alexander's dream, the same dream coveted by Caesar and Augustus: uniform customs and laws uniting West and East. There remained the problem of citizenship, which was granted only rarely and with many limitations. The conquered peoples were not content to play the role of spectators and demanded equal rights. Trajan, the first emperor from the provinces, launched the provincials' climb to power, to high government offices and magistracies, and even to the throne. Their fellow countrymen, as they celebrated and honored these

THE ROMAN EMPIRE
Under Trajan, the empire achieved its maximum expansion. From Britain to Spain and from Africa to Syria, millions of people were under Roman dominion.

The frontiers
The frontiers were garrisoned by auxiliary troops in order to observe the movements of unsubdued tribes and to repel sudden attacks, while the legions were stationed in the interior, ready to intervene at a moment's notice.

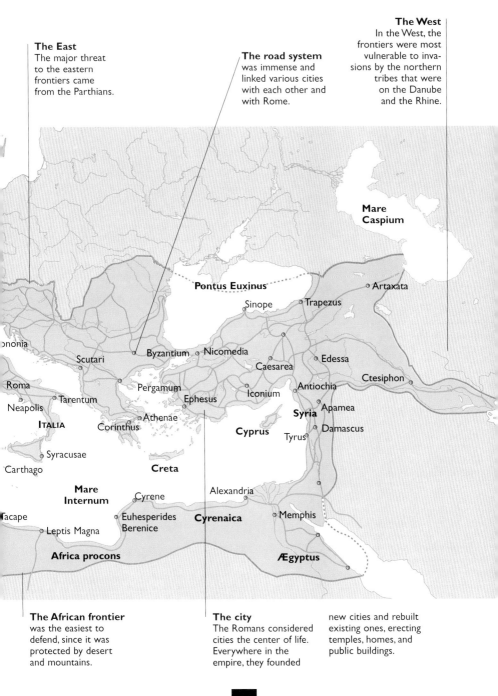

The East
The major threat to the eastern frontiers came from the Parthians.

The road system
was immense and linked various cities with each other and with Rome.

The West
In the West, the frontiers were most vulnerable to invasions by the northern tribes that were on the Danube and the Rhine.

Mare
Caspium

Pontus Euxinus

Artaxata

Sinope   Trapezus

ɔnonia

Scutari   Byzantium   Nicomedia   Edessa

Caesarea   Ctesiphon

Roma   Pergamum   Antiochia

Neapolis   Tarentum   Ephesus   Iconium   Apamea

ITALIA   Athenae   Syria   Damascus

Corinthus   Cyprus   Tyrus

Syracusae   Creta

Carthago

Mare Internum   Cyrene   Alexandria

Tacape   Euhesperides   Cyrenaica   Memphis
Berenice

Leptis Magna

Africa procons   **Ægyptus**

The African frontier
was the easiest to defend, since it was protected by desert and mountains.

The city
The Romans considered cities the center of life. Everywhere in the empire, they founded

new cities and rebuilt existing ones, erecting temples, homes, and public buildings.

figures, realized that they too would be able to rise to the top. Therefore, while Rome was spreading its culture and transforming the peoples it had conquered, it also instilled in them an awareness of their own possibilities, especially in the East that could not and would not forget its grand and ancient culture.

Hadrian: The architect emperor

Trajan's successor, Aelius Hadrianus, who reigned from A.D. 117 to 138, was also Spanish, and is remembered as a man of culture. The many problems at the borders of the empire led Hadrian to enact a policy of consolidation. He preferred to renounce some territories rather than overex-

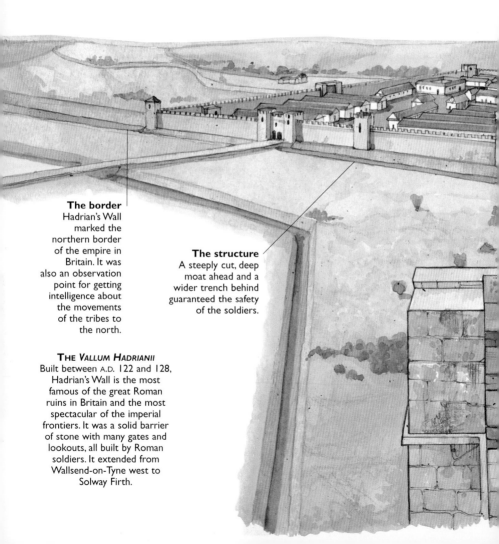

The border
Hadrian's Wall marked the northern border of the empire in Britain. It was also an observation point for getting intelligence about the movements of the tribes to the north.

The structure
A steeply cut, deep moat ahead and a wider trench behind guaranteed the safety of the soldiers.

THE VALLUM HADRIANII
Built between A.D. 122 and 128, Hadrian's Wall is the most famous of the great Roman ruins in Britain and the most spectacular of the imperial frontiers. It was a solid barrier of stone with many gates and lookouts, all built by Roman soldiers. It extended from Wallsend-on-Tyne west to Solway Firth.

tend the empire in exhausting wars. He abandoned Armenia, Mesopotamia, and Assyria. Possessed with insatiable curiosity and fascinated by the exotic, he traveled at length to all parts of the empire for a firsthand look at the masterpieces of Greek and Hellenistic art, which inspired his great architectural works. His nickname "Architect Emperor" comes from his untiring construction throughout the empire. He designed and built his villa in Tivoli, an extraordinary complex of buildings including baths, theaters, fountains, and public squares and terraces all surrounded and interspersed with lush green areas. He built his mausoleum

Life on the Wall was hard, especially in winter. Hadrian's Wall and its forts were garrisoned by more than 11,000 soldiers.

in Rome, rebuilt a large part of the city of Athens, and filled the provinces with splendid edifices. Hadrian's travels, however, also demonstrated, with his physical presence, that Rome made no distinction among the peoples of the empire, and that Italians and provincials were equal in the sight of the emperor. He did not stop here; he also worked to create, among the inhabitants of the provinces, elements suitable for holding offices in local, provincial, and imperial government, spurred on by the need to integrate those human resources that by his time had become noticeably depleted. The ancient power struggle with the Senate, always ready to affirm its independence, became stronger. Hadrian's solution was to impose imperial authority.

Anubis
The Egyptian jackal-headed god of death and the afterlife.

THE ORIENTAL RELIGIONS
The Oriental religions spread and gained favor in Rome because they satisfied the intellectual and spiritual needs of individuals. The new gods contrasted with those of the traditional Roman divinities, and over the course of the centuries contributed to changing the face of Roman religious tradition.

Two extraordinary emperors

Hadrian's successors, Antoninus Pius and Marcus Aurelius, were wise and just emperors. Antoninus, who ascended the throne in A.D. 138, was a native of Gaul. His great tolerance and devotion to justice earned him the unofficial title of "Pius" from the Senate. Unlike Hadrian, he gave great freedom to the Senate in matters of government, and although he never left Rome to check on the provinces, he continued the work of peacefully consolidating the borders of the empire. There were no wars during his reign, only unimportant skirmishes. It was different for his successor Marcus Aurelius. Although he longed for peace, he was forced to fight at length. After having faced the Parthians and retaken Mesopotamia, he fought the Quadi and the Marcomanni, two

Isis and Osiris
The cult of Isis and her consort Osiris originated in Egypt and soon spread throughout the Mediterranean, reaching Rome about the first century B.C.

Mithraism
originated in Persia and spread to Rome through Asia Minor in the first century A.D. Mithras was the god of light, in constant opposition to the evil prince of darkness.

Immortality
These cults were based on the doctrine of immortality and therefore contributed to calming individuals' fear of death. Osiris, for example, died and was resurrected to permit his wife Isis to conceive their son Horus.

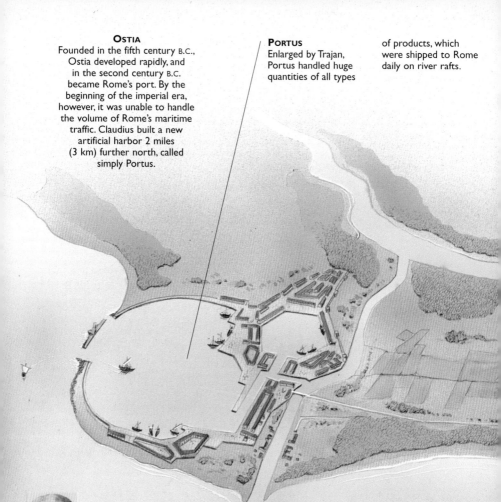

OSTIA
Founded in the fifth century B.C.,
Ostia developed rapidly, and
in the second century B.C.
became Rome's port. By the
beginning of the imperial era,
however, it was unable to handle
the volume of Rome's maritime
traffic. Claudius built a new
artificial harbor 2 miles
(3 km) further north, called
simply Portus.

PORTUS
Enlarged by Trajan,
Portus handled huge
quantities of all types
of products, which
were shipped to Rome
daily on river rafts.

Germanic peoples who lived north of the Danube. This war began the empire's struggles against the barbarian hordes that, in the centuries that followed, led to the collapse of the great Roman state. The educated and tolerant Marcus Aurelius, a disciple of Stoic philosophy (earning him the nick-name of "Philosopher Emperor"), always showed great respect for the Senate. His reign is remembered as a time of great prosperity and well-being. The 60 years from Hadrian to Marcus Aurelius were the happiest in the history of Rome. The Roman world enjoyed a long period of peace. New, well-designed cities full of

The products
The port of Ostia berthed ships from the Orient loaded with slaves and amber, and ships from the North carrying furs. Other ships transported gold, wood, and ivory from North Africa.

Rome
In the second century B.C., Rome was a city with a population of one million. Since it was substantially unproductive, its inhabitants depended on imports for their needs.

Ostia

grand monuments were founded and built up, trade blossomed, agricultural activities developed, and culture received new stimuli. The standard of living in the provinces, even the furthest, increased and came to resemble that of Rome.

The situation changed under Commodus, the son of Marcus Aurelius who ascended the throne in A.D. 180. He was tyrannical and dissolute, and was assassinated in A.D. 193. His death was followed by a period of anarchy in which the dominant element was once again military strength. It was this renewed importance of the army that was to change the form of government in Rome.

THE SLOW DECLINE OF THE EMPIRE

The third century A.D. was the beginning of a period of military anarchy, invasions, and economic and financial crises. After a phase of recovery, the eastern part of the empire split from the western part, which was conquered by the Germanic invasions of the fifth century A.D.

Even at its height, the empire already contained the seeds of crisis. This became evident at the death of Commodus, when every army stationed at the borders elected its own emperor. The armies were made up mostly of inhabitants of the provinces, a situation brought about mainly by Hadrian's reforms, and the various armies, each with deep-rooted ties to its garrison, had lost any awareness of imperial unity.

Septimius Severus, an African general whose power was based solely on the army, won out at the central level. Paying only lip service to the Senate, he transformed the empire into a military monarchy and reinforced its borders, which were sorely threatened by barbarian tribes. He was one of those

A CHANGING WORLD
This period of great crisis for the empire affected Roman life and art. A transformation came about in sculpture where the faces began to reflect the generalized sense of anxiety and dissatisfaction.

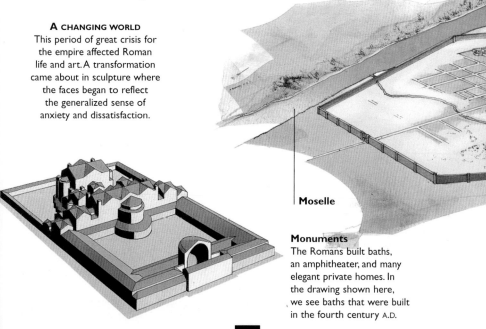

Moselle

Monuments
The Romans built baths, an amphitheater, and many elegant private homes. In the drawing shown here, we see baths that were built in the fourth century A.D.

provincials who had acquired a keen awareness of his own abilities. He therefore attempted to make all the peoples of the empire equal by eliminating the privileges of the Italian population. This policy was continued by his son Caracalla, who in A.D. 212 granted Roman citizenship to all the inhabitants of the provinces. The Severan dynasty upheld the empire until 235, when it met a violent end upon the assasination of Alexander Severus. Fifty years of military anarchy began, with a series of emperors elected by the various legions. The last emperors of this era, natives of the Balkans and therefore called Illyrians, attempted to resolve the crisis. Aurelian, who reigned from 270 to 275, surrounded Rome with the great walls that still bear his name.

Trier (Treveris) was the ancient capital of the Treveri, a people of Celtic-Germanic orgin. It took the name of Augusta Trevirorum on the occasion of Augustus's visit during his trip to Gaul in 15–13 B.C.

A fortunate position
In the early days of the empire, Treveris prospered because it was close to a waterway that provided access to the Rhine fortifications. In the third century, its prestige grew when it became the principal imperial residence in the West.

The city plan
As rebuilt by Augustus, Treveris's city plan was styled on the typical Roman grid layout.

The Black Gate
To enter the north side of Treveri, one had to cross the majestic Black Gate. Dating from the fourth century A.D. it is formed by two doors united by a three-story gallery.

The decline of the West and the rise of the East

During the two centuries of the principate, huge sums of money were spent in prestigious but unprofitable construction, such as forums, temples, theaters, and amphitheaters. In the third century A.D., the empire experienced a crisis that changed all aspects of social life. The pressure brought to bear by the barbarians on the western border and by the Parthians to the East was a continual threat. The army, which had become increasingly greedy and powerful, absorbed the majority of the resources of the state, which was then forced to increase taxes. Uninterrupted war and a burdensome fiscal policy brought the economic situation to a head. Agriculture, the principal resource of the West, declined, due particularly to a decrease in slavery, which made it more difficult to procure the needed farm laborers.

The social order of the age of the principate had broken down. In that time, the upper classes—the senatorial order, the *equites*, and the decurionate—were the epitome of power, wealth, and prestige. Beginning in the third century, these functions and privileges began to crumble. The members of the senatorial order remained very rich, but they had less and less power. The power of the soldiers increased, however, and they organized themselves as though they were a true social order. In fact, the crisis produced the great soldier-emperors of the last third of the third century, thanks to the growing strength of the military and

EPHESUS, THE MARVEL OF THE ORIENT
Ephesus was one of the most important cities in Asia Minor. In the late second century B.C., it was taken by the Romans, who made it the capital of the province of Asia.

The facade was decorated with alcoves containing statues of Wisdom, Virtue, Intelligence, and Science.

The Library of Celsus was built between A.D. 110 and 135 by the consul Julius Aquila in honor of his father Julius Celsus.

The great hall was 52 feet (16 m) high and 36 feet (11 m) wide. The floor and the walls, decorated with bas-reliefs, were entirely in marble.

Books

The library could hold up to 12,000 parchments on shelves set in alcoves. Each book was written by hand by an expert copyist, who transcribed the words dictated by an assistant, who, in turn, read the original work or, more often, an eariler copy. Each manuscript was therefore the result of many days of work.

bureaucratic machines. But the real victims of the crisis were the lowerclass masses, the *humiliores* (humble ones). Their misery and poverty were made worse by famine and terrible epidemics that decimated the population. Because it became increasingly difficult to find men for the army among the people of the empire, barbarians were allowed within its borders. They were even granted land to cultivate if they agreed to fight for the empire. Agriculture, commerce, and industry continued to prosper in the East, and the great ancient cities such as Ephesus and Alexandria became major cultural and trade centers of the empire. This was the climate in which Christianity gained a foothold and spread in the third century.

Empire vs. Christianity

The empire, generally tolerant toward all religions, often persecuted Christians. Diocletian, in particular, began years of persecution, imprisoning and martyring many Christians, and destroying places of worship. Acclaimed emperor by his soldiers in A.D. 285, the Illyrian general Diocletian succeeded in reestablishing central authority after many decades of chaos and anarchy. Realizing that one man alone could not hope to keep control of all the borders of the empire, he divided up command among two Augusti and two Caesars. This was the tetrarchy, a system that, although it solved the immediate problem, was eventually a further cause of the decline of the West. For the time being, however,

Places of concealment?
The idea that the Christians hid in the catacombs to escape persecution is unfounded. It would have been impossible for many people to hide there for any length of time.

THE CATACOMBS
were underground cemeteries whose only functions were to preserve Christian corpses and host the liturgical ceremonies commemorating their lives.

Burial
A martyr was carried
through the subterranean
passages and, after a funeral
ceremony, was entombed.

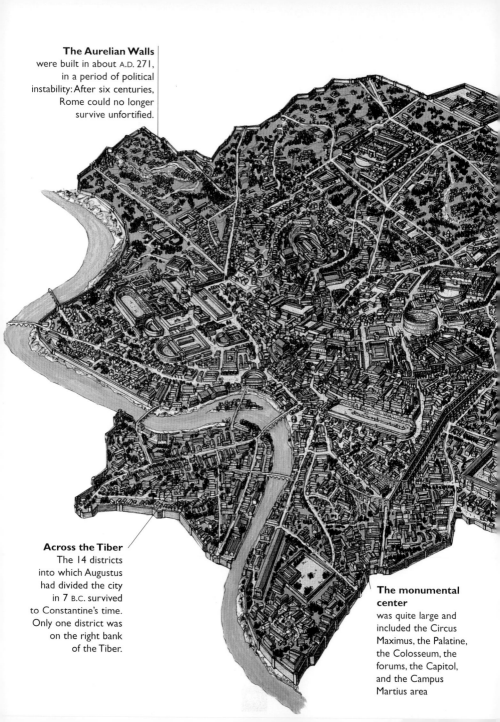

The Aurelian Walls
were built in about A.D. 271,
in a period of political
instability: After six centuries,
Rome could no longer
survive unfortified.

Across the Tiber
The 14 districts
into which Augustus
had divided the city
in 7 B.C. survived
to Constantine's time.
Only one district was
on the right bank
of the Tiber.

**The monumental
center**
was quite large and
included the Circus
Maximus, the Palatine,
the Colosseum, the
forums, the Capitol,
and the Campus
Martius area

Rome's urban structure reflected enormous internal contradictions: areas where power and wealth resided, with their splended monuments, poor districts where there was abject misery and degredation, and the countryside, forced to bear the burden of supporting an increasingly overpopulated city.

Surface area
The Aurelian Walls surrounded an area of 3,423 acres (1,386 ha) in which the population density was the highest in the Western world.

The district registers
counted 1,790 domas and 44,300 insulae in Rome.

The center of Rome
The districts fanned out from the Meta Sudante fountain near the Colosseum. It was the center of Rome.

Diocletian succeeded in defending his frontiers and putting down the revolts that had broken out everywhere. At the same time, he reorganized and strengthened the army, the bureaucracy, and the tax offices. He invested imperial authority with great religious significance capable of swaying the masses, who, above all in the East, were accustomed to thinking of their ruler as a god. This was why he persecuted the Christians, who, although acknowledging the authority of the emperor, refused to worship him. Diocletian remained in power for more than 20 years, and during this time he succeeded in reinforcing the state, but also created serious causes for its division. For example, he created a powerful and privileged class of bureaucrats and estate holders, and granted autonomy to certain parts of the empire. Constantine, his successor, found much to keep him occupied when he ascended the throne.

Constantine

When he came to power in 312, Constantine immediately countermanded Diocletian's policy toward Christianity. He granted freedom of worship in 313 and, well aware of the power of the new religion, made a place for Christianity in the structure of the Roman state, granting it broad privileges. The religious unity of the Church was at the time threatened by heretics. Constantine promoted the Nicene Council in 325 to define the fundamental doctrines of the religion, which are still in force today in

The *Amphiteatrum Flavium* or the Colosseum, with its magnificence and immense size, was a grandiose scenario for imperial triumphs.

Population In the early fourth century, Rome numbered about one million inhabitants. It was at the apex of a period of intense construction activity in the wake of a number of reforms.

Catholicism and Orthodoxy. Next, he abolished the tetrarchic system and took over control of the entire empire. He also created the basic premise for the future division into West and East, when he transferred the capital of the empire. Ancient Byzantium, on the Bosphorus, was enlarged, embellished, and "refounded" as Constantinople. The consequences of this were incredibly far-reaching. The government of the empire as a whole took on a Greek-Hellenistic cast. Partly because of its great past and much more because it was the site of the ministry and martyrdom of Saint Peter and Saint Paul, Rome became the most important

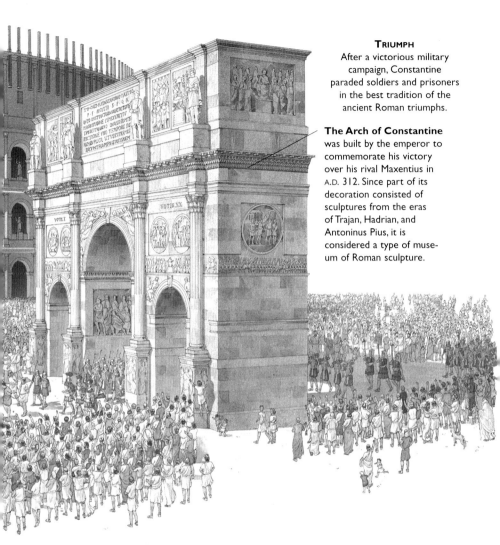

episcopal see in all Christendom. At Constantine's death in 337, the unity of the empire was more formal than real; imperial power was based on a powerful group of bureaucrats and a close-knit circle of large landowners, on military leaders who were often of barbarian origin, and on a few Christian bishops.

The division of the Empire

In 379, Theodosius, a military commander of Spanish origin, succeeded Valens, who was defeated and killed in battle by the Visigoths, and infused the empire with new vigor. Theodosius's Edict of Thessalonike (380) declared Christianity the official religion of the empire. During his reign, there was an event that introduced something new into the history of western Europe. In Thessalonike, in Macedonia, in order to crush a rebellion by the Goths, Theodosius had ordered reprisals against the people who had earlier caused uprisings, during which a Gothic general had been killed. The great bishop of Milan, Ambrose, excommunicated Theodosius for the massacre, and imposed a penitence on the emperor. This event illustrates how power was shifting, with the Church becoming more authoritative than even the head of the Roman government.

Before Theodosius died in 395, he showed he understood the extreme delicacy of the situation by assigning the West to his young son, Honorius, and the East to his elder son, Arcadius, thus laying the foundation for the formation of two parts of the empire. The eastern part of the empire was stronger and better organized, and indeed continued for over a millennium. The western part of the empire, however, was destined to dissolve within a few decades under the pressure of barbarian invasions.

The end of the western part of the Roman Empire

It was the ability to stand up to the barbarians that made all the difference. In the East, an energetic policy had prevented barbarians or their descendants from securing high military and government posts, and during the reign of Theodosius II (408–450), Constantinople was surrounded by

CONSTANTINOPLE
The great city built by Constantine and inaugurated on May 11, A.D. 330 grew at a surprising rate. The available financial resources were practically unlimited, and Constantine could count on craftsmen and materials flowing in from all over the East. The city had a Senate and was home to one of the two imperial consuls. It was divided into 14 districts, exactly like Rome. The streets and buildings had an amazing number of statues and ornaments.

The basilica, on a nearly square plan, is topped by an elongated dome and two half-domes at the sides. The interior is well lighted by large windows, and the walls are richly adorned with engraved decorations and mosaics.

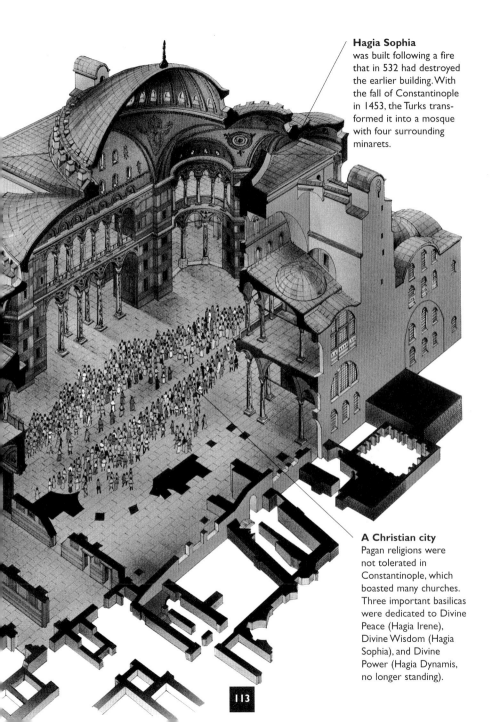

Hagia Sophia
was built following a fire
that in 532 had destroyed
the earlier building. With
the fall of Constantinople
in 1453, the Turks trans-
formed it into a mosque
with four surrounding
minarets.

A Christian city
Pagan religions were
not tolerated in
Constantinople, which
boasted many churches.
Three important basilicas
were dedicated to Divine
Peace (Hagia Irene),
Divine Wisdom (Hagia
Sophia), and Divine
Power (Hagia Dynamis,
no longer standing).

113

THE GERMANS
were a group of peoples of
common culture and language.
They settled east of the Rhine
and north of the Danube, but
had to abandon their land
under pressure from other
barbarian populations, in
particular the Huns.

walls that kept it from being captured for centuries. The West, instead, in the fifth century, suffered an irreversible collapse. Its immense bureaucratic-military machine, no longer supported by public funds, ground to a standstill. Honorius, fearing for his life, moved his residence from Rome to Ravenna.

Despite the victories of the great general Stilicho, who in 414 succeeded in stopping the Visigoths at the eastern Italian border, the Rhine frontier forts fell in 406 and Alamanni, Burgundians, Swabians, Franks, and Vandals raged into France and the Iberian peninsula. The city of Rome was sacked twice (a

Religion
was based on the forces of nature and warrior traditions.

The economy
was based on herding and agriculture, supplemented by hunting and raiding.

Laws
The Germanic peoples had no law other than their customs, and their only way to settle disputes was the feud, or private justice.

Barbarian society was based on family clans, called *sippe* or *fara*. The king was the military commander and the freemen, the *arimanni*, were soldiers. Those who did not carry arms were considered servants.

fact unheard of until then), by Alaric's Goths in 410 and by Genseric's Vandals in 455. Enormous tracts of land were run over and destroyed by the barbarians, who met with no resistance. It is said that the most terrible raid, that of Attila's Huns, was stopped by Pope Leo I, who stood before the Hun unarmed as a man of God. Some of the barbarians settled permanently in different areas of the empire: the Vandals in Africa, the Visigoths in Spain, the Franks in Gaul, and the Saxons and Angles in Britain.

Italy managed to avoid being settled by great numbers of barbarians, but could not avoid the decline of the empire, which finally fell in 476

Justinian I wanted to restore the empire to its ancient grandeur. He undertook to unite all Roman law in a single code.

The *Corpus iuris civilis* Composed in five books, its goal was to combine ancient law with the imperial legislation that followed.

when the barbarian leader Odoacer deposed Romulus Augustulus, the last emperor. From that moment on, the western part of the Roman Empire ceased to exist. The year 476 conventionally marks the passage from the ancient era to the Dark Ages.

Italy and the Orient

Odoacer's reign did not last long: Italy was overrun by Theodoric's Ostrogoths, who entered Ravenna in 493. Close to the eastern part of the empire in terms both of geography—the Ostrogoths came from the Balkan peninsula—and of religion, they were pushed toward Italy by the emperor in Constantinople, who wanted to be rid of them.

Theodoric's kingdom was one of the most important among those set up by the barbarians in the West. These dominions were called Roman-Barbarian kingdoms, because the ancient Roman traditions lived on in the bureaucratic and administrative structures and in the spirit of the laws. Justinian, who ascended the Roman throne in 525, was a fine figure of an emperor, who attempted to reunify the empire. He succeeded, although for only a brief period. In 568, Italy was invaded by the Lombards, a new Germanic people from the East. The Lombard civilization was backward, but gradually they were assimilated and converted to Christianity. Thus, in the early eighth century, the great king Liudprand pledged material aid to the Church of Rome and promised to augment its territorial and political power

Compiling the Justinian Code
Justinian entrusted the work to eminent jurists who, with the help and under the direction of the minister Trebonian, worked on it from 519 to 534.

in exchange for acknowledgment of Lombard rule in Italy. This agreement weakened at the death of Liudprand, whose successors, aware of the fact that the pope was destined to become the center of forces hostile to their kingdom, openly threatened the Church of Rome, which then turned to the Franks for aid.

The Carolingian empire

In what is modern France, the Franks had established the largest and most populous of the barbarian kingdoms. In 774, their king Charles, known in history as Charlemagne, defeated the Lombards and annexed their territories, including a large part of Italy. Charles's power grew to the point that he was able to con-

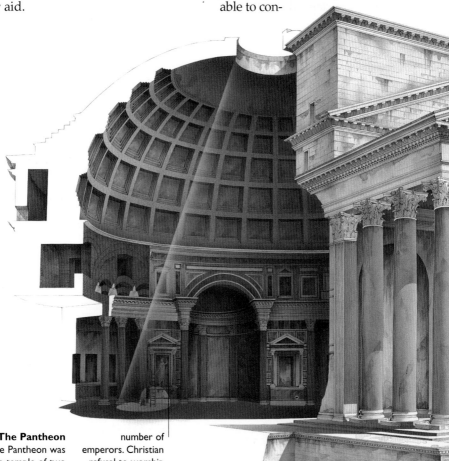

The Pantheon
The Pantheon was the temple of two divinities, Venus and Mars, and also held the statues of a number of emperors. Christian refusal to worship the emperor was one reason they were persecuted.

quer almost all of central Europe. He was also a man of strong faith. Pope Leo III therefore took what was to prove a step of enormous historical importance. He created an emperor capable of uniting all the Christian peoples of the West and protecting the Church from its enemies. Charles's coronation took place on Christmas in the year 800, when the pope solemnly proclaimed him Roman emperor of a territory that extended from the Pyrenees to eastern Germany, and from the North Sea to the Mediterranean. This enormous area, because of the divine significance attributed by the Church to the union, from then on was called the Roman Empire. In 912, another German emperor, Otto I, was crowned by a pope. This empire is known as the Holy Roman Empire.

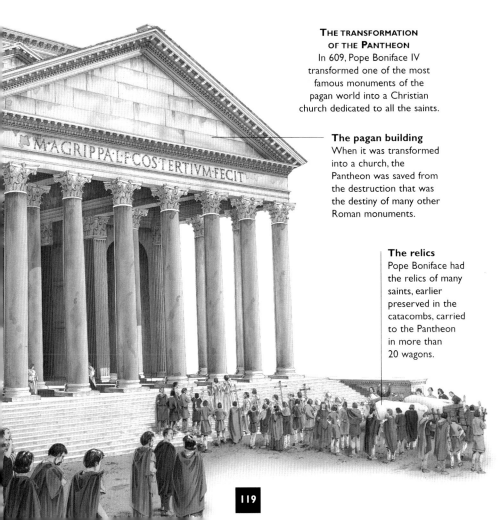

THE TRANSFORMATION OF THE PANTHEON
In 609, Pope Boniface IV transformed one of the most famous monuments of the pagan world into a Christian church dedicated to all the saints.

The pagan building
When it was transformed into a church, the Pantheon was saved from the destruction that was the destiny of many other Roman monuments.

The relics
Pope Boniface had the relics of many saints, earlier preserved in the catacombs, carried to the Pantheon in more than 20 wagons.

Index

ACKNOWLEDGMENTS

The illustrations displayed in this volume are new and original. They have been realized upon a project by DoGi s.p.a. that owns its copyright.

ILLUSTRATIONS:
Alessandro Baldanzi: 16–17, 60–61, 68–69, 96–97; Alessandro Bartolozzi: 4–5, 22–23, 28–29 (map), 100–101; Giovanni Bernardi: 76–77; Lorenzo Cecchi: 28–29 (pictures), 38–39, 38, 64–65, 82–83; Piergiorgio Citterio: 108–109; Paolo Donati: 54–55; Luigi Galante: 57; Giacinto Gaudenzi: 92–93; Roberto Lari: 52–53; Francesco Lo Bello: 62–63; 102–103; Bernardo Mannucci (computer artworks): 8, 94–95; Andrea Ricciardi: 14–15; 34–35, 88–89, 118–119; Claudia Saraceni: 84–85, 104–105, 116–117; Sergio: 8–9, 20–21, 26–27, 40–41, 42, 46–47, 50–51, 86–87, 91, 98–99, 102–103, 114–115; Giacomo Soriani: 10–11, 18–19, 30–31, 36–37, 42–43, 58–59, 74–75, 80–81, 90–91; Ivan Stalio: 112–113; Studio Inklink: 6–7, 12–13, 24–25, 44bl, 44tr, 48–49, 56, 70–71, 78–79, 106–107, 110–111; Sansai Zappini (computer artworks): 41b, 60, 73;

REPRODUCTIONS AND DOCUMENTS:
DoGi s.p.a. has done its best to discover possible rights of third parties. We apologize for any omissions or mistakes that might have occurred, and we will be pleased to introduce the appropriate corrections in the later editions of this book.
Aldus Archive/Syndication International: 15; Archaeological Museum, Florence: 13l, 13r; Arris/ Araldo De Luca, Rome: 59, 66c, 67l; Bibliotheque Nationale, Paris: 36; Bildkunstverlag Gerard/Waltraud Klammet: 81; Dagli Orti, Paris: 10; De Antonio, Rome: 28; DoGi Archives, Florence: 6, 7, 21, 23l, 32l, 33t, 33b, 82, 83, 91, 99; Hirmer Fotoarchiv, Munich: 32r; Louvre Museum, Paris: 45tl, 51; Luisa Ricciarini Agency: 45tr, 45b, 56b; Michael Vickers: 35; Münzkabinett, Berlin: 73l; Panini, Modena: 66tr; Pedicini: 73br; Quilici, Rome: 25; Ronald Sheridan: 50; Rossenbach/ Zefa: 103; Scala Archives, Florence: 66tl, 72, 92, 93, 98; V.D.F. La Phototheque: 23t, 23b, 44t, 67r, 76, 85; Valsecchi, Florence: 34, 47

Cover: Studio Inklink
Frontispiece: Andrea Ricciardi
Abbreviations: t: top/b: below/c: center/r: right/l: left.